CHRISTIAN CHURCH ART THROUGH THE AGES

THE MACMILLAN COMPANY
NEW YORK • CHICAGO
DALLAS • ATLANTA • SAN FRANCISCO
LONDON • MANILA

IN CANADA
BRETT-MACMILLAN LTD.
GALT, ONTARIO

CHRISTIAN CHURCH ART THROUGH THE AGES

by

Katharine Morrison McClinton

New York
THE MACMILLAN COMPANY
1962

First Printing

The Macmillan Company, New York
Brett-Macmillan Ltd., Galt, Ontario

Printed in the United States of America

Library of Congress catalog card number: 62-7245

In Appreciation

Katharine Morrison McClinton, in her book on Christian art, has proved to be very direct and forthright in getting at the heart of the subject she is discussing. She certainly presents the idea, the spirit, the character peculiar to the subject, and the differences between varying manifestations of the Christian arts. She has made her comprehensive story very clear.

We are given the big, significant elements, and enough of detail of the lesser, yet telling, material. She well exemplifies the manifold features of the survey.

Each of the fine arts, that is, the major arts, like architecture, sculpture, and painting, has its day; however, the so-called minor arts are not neglected. She gives us indeed a great deal, considering the necessary restrictions of a book that treats of this seemingly endless subject. She has the gift of writing concisely, and in an uncomplicated way, even concerning this very complicated material. Her presentation is vivid; and, as we read, we feel a certain warmth. She presents a true picture, at the same time giving us her own summation of the subject.

Her exposition is clear, clean-cut, and easily grasped by the reader. The character of the presentation is attractive, intriguing, appealing—it makes one wish to delve further and deeper into this wonderful theme. This story of Christian art makes good reading. It is a delightful, exciting, and stimulating exposition of one of life's greatest movements: Christian art.

DR. REGINALD POLAND
Director of Museums
Atlanta Art Association
Atlanta, Georgia

Preface

In the study of art, appreciation is more important than history or dates or the understanding of art styles. It is not enough to know about art. Art must be experienced. Works of art speak to us, appeal to us, and act on us as living entities. Thus it is my purpose to introduce the reader to the experience of enjoying art so that he can not only feel the grandeur of the Byzantine mosaics but also the lyric beauty of a Blake water color and the decorative appeal of the intertwinings of a cruciform page in the Book of Kells or the Lindisfarne Gospels. These pleasures are too seldom experienced.

The study of art should also lead to the understanding and appreciation of art of all countries and all ages as well as all mediums of expression; the threads of likeness, unity, and continuity of art expression should be emphasized. Each work of art must not only be made understandable in terms of its singular background and the intention of the artist who created it but also of its place in the unity of the whole field of art.

The story of art is not divided into separate chapters, although such divisions are necessary in a book. Art is a universal language that has different accents and variations according to the artist, his nationality, and his period in history. But a certain continuity binds all art together.

Recognition of the rhythmic vitality and expressive value at the heart of a work of art has led to a revaluation of the art of the ages. Thus El Greco was brought out of obscurity into the top rank of old masters as critics became aware of the intensity and mystic quality of his work. Similarly, the rhythmic vitality of Romanesque painting and sculpture has finally brought it long overdue recognition. Through recent research a continuing stream of profoundly creative art down through the ages has been uncovered and brought to notice, while many old favorites are now given second place or dropped altogether from the lists of great art.

With the present-day awakening of religious leaders to the value of art and its place in the Church, it seems timely that the religious art of the past should also be revalued. Its new aspects and significance should be made known in the light of present-day Christianity as well as in the thinking of today's art experts.

This book attempts to open up the path and give a panoramic view of Christian art, to define the qualities of art, and to call attention to art that has Christian values. It is not the purpose to trace history but to point out the development of the religious theme as shown by the greatest examples. Thus, in a period where artists and their works are legion we shall be selective and choose the most significant portrayals of the Christian theme. The history of art shows us that what determines the character and the subject matter of art is the nature of the religious belief, or lack of belief, of the age. Christian art reflects the changing views that different ages have held regarding the representation of transcendental truth in a work of art. Our interest here centers on how artists of the past expressed their Christian experience and faith and how we today can interpret our faith through the medium of art.

As the world becomes "one world" and we work toward "one Church," so the art of all time and of all places grows closer and closer together. But this universal quality has always existed in art. Thus, Byzantine, which contains so much Eastern influence, is a branch of Classic Greek art. The influence of the Greek appears in the Celtic art of the British Isles, and the dancing figures of Angkor Vat are seen on the portals of French Romanesque churches. The universal cosmic rhythm that permeates all nature is also present in all great art, and the story of art is dominated by the artist's desire to hold fast and reveal the universal life in an image that will define it for all time.

The manuscript was read in part by Dr. A. Howard Meneely, President of Wheaton College, Norton, Massachusetts; Dr. Reginald Poland, Director of Museums, Atlanta Art Association, Atlanta, Georgia; The Rev. John La Farge, S. J.; Robert Laurer, Associate Director of the Museum of Contemporary Crafts, New York City; and Theodore Rousseau, Jr., Curator of Painting, the Metropolitan Museum of Art. I wish to thank them all for their encouragement and constructive and generally approving criticism. I wish to thank Robert Laurer especially for his assistance with data concerning the work of American and European craftsmen. Finally, I owe a special indebtedness to Dr. Reginald Poland for his suggestions concerning illustrations and for writing the Preface.

In a book of this nature there is a certain indebtedness to past and present writers of general histories, and the enthusiasm and literary appeal of Élie Faure, René Huyghe, and André Malraux gave inspiration. But my indebtedness is even more to the specialists of each period.

For specific aid in procuring photographs, I wish to thank Janet S. Byrne, Associate Curator of the Print Department, Metropolitan Museum of Art; Margaret Witherspoon of the National Sculpture Society; Dorothea Denslow, Director of the Sculpture Center; the British Information Service; Services Culturels Français; the German Tourist Information Service; the National Council of Churches; the Belgium Government Information Center; the Irish Consulate General; and each individual artist who supplied photographs. I also wish to thank the staffs of the Art Division of the New York Public Library and the Library of the Metropolitan Museum of Art.

Contents

Illustrations

(Plates I-XVI follow page 80; Plates XVII-XLVIII follow page 112; Plates XLIX-LXIV follow page 144.)

Beauty is truth, truth beauty,—that is all
Ye know on earth, and all ye need to know.
—JOHN KEATS, *"Ode on a Grecian Urn"*

CHAPTER I

ART AND CHRISTIANITY

That art is best which to the soul's range gives no bound.
Something besides the form, something beyond the sound.

Both art and religion are expressions of man's sense of the spiritual significance of the universe. Both are human attempts to express things unseen and eternal; both are means to unearthly states of mind. In the words of Clive Bell, "art and religion are then, two roads by which men escape from circumstance to ecstasy." In music, poetry, color, and design, the artist creates harmonies that are able to express values of religion, rhythms of prayer, and even the intangible beauty of holiness. For the artist's unique gift is to see beyond the narrow reality of the moment into the breadth of eternity. Through art, religion takes on a new dimension. Similarly, the art lover can be freed from matter so that his spirit transcends himself and moves in the rhythm of things. "It is thus that art becomes akin to religion and ennobles mankind," according to Kakuzo Okakura in *The Book of Tea.*

Nearly everyone knows the closer kinship with God that comes from viewing a beautiful sunset or looking up at the stars in the evening sky or watching the endless roll of ocean waves or flying above the clouds. "If I take the wings of the morning, and dwell in the uttermost parts of the sea; Even there shall thy hand lead me, and thy right hand shall hold me" (Psalm 139:9–10). But not only nature produces this effect. Who is not elevated toward the infinite through music such as Handel's *Messiah* or *Creation* or such hymns as "Holy, Holy, Holy"? Or who is not moved by the luminous beauty of the stained glass in the windows of Chartres or Notre-Dame or Amiens?

"For there is music wherever there is harmony, order, or proportion, and thus far we maintain the music of the spheres," said Sir Thomas Browne in *Religio Medici.*

Thus in these different fields the artist's sensitive perception can increase our religious fervor, for the artist has the power of expressing the infinite. According to the eighteenth century poet and artist William Blake, poetry, painting, and music are "the three powers in man of conversing with Paradise." The artist can also point out truths and beauties that we have not hitherto seen or perhaps imperfectly understood. A great picture, such as Grünewald's "Resurrection," or sculpture, such as Donatello's "St. John the Baptist," can implant a truth that even the most eloquent sermon cannot communicate. If the object of art supplements Bible reading, the lesson can be implanted both through the ear and through the eye, and the mind will have a double impression.

In past ages the Church made extensive use of the visual arts in teaching the Christian religion. Because few people in the early Church could read, what could be seen assumed great importance. Early Christianity—its teachings, dogma, and history—were put in the form of painting, mosaic, and sculpture decorating the walls, ceilings, and even the floors of churches so that all could see. These works of art became the people's Bible.

The loss of contact between the Protestant Church and the arts during the Reformation is well known. The Church today is seeking a rapprochement with art, especially with music and the drama. But the plastic and other visual arts are still neglected by the majority of churches and are unappreciated by the average churchgoer. When we study religious art at all, it is usually only religious painting. The habit of treating the history of art as primarily the history of painting can give us only a part of the story. To be complete, the history of art of any era should be concerned with every medium, with sculpture as well as painting, with the small articles of everyday usage, as well as great showpieces, and with architecture, which is so important in the history of the art of the Christian Church. Especially is this true in the early Church, where the buildings and their decorative arts had an over-all unity and religious significance.

Our appreciation of the visual arts of the Church has been confined mainly to paintings and to pictures of one or two periods, with emphasis on the nineteenth century painters or the great masters of the Renaissance. We have limited our enjoyment of Church art to these one or two periods and one or two mediums, and have left the vast richness of Christian art and iconography to the concern of the museum and the art historian while the Church "fasts" from art.

One does not find the whole story of an era in a history of the Christian religion, or the whole story of art in a history of art, but the two are intermingled. To get the complete picture and full enjoyment, both must be studied. And in the study we enlarge our heritage of the Christian understanding of life.

The Church and people of the Church have much to gain from exploring the vast treasure of Christian art. Fully to understand and experience religion and to reap our own rich inheritance we should study all periods of the development of Christian art. Of special value are the art expressions of the early Church from the fourth century to the eighth century when religious feeling was at its height of intensity. A great amount of our knowledge of the ancient Church would be lost except for the testimony of the art of these times, and this art also has much to interest and inspire us.

The vast historic background of the Church is continually being revealed by discoveries of archaeologists digging in Italy, Palestine, and Asia Minor. Just recently the discovery of the Dead Sea Scrolls has helped to bring the intertestamental period alive by giving us a closer view of the life of the ancient days that cradled the New Testament. Archaeology reveals and authenticates the historical side of the Bible, but only the artist can interpret and reveal the spiritual meaning and bring to life Biblical passages.

Small articles of everyday life of early Christian times help to bring us in contact with the life and people of Bible times and thus enlarge and broaden our understanding and enjoyment of the Bible. For the average person, how much more directly is the contact with Bible times revealed in a little African Christian terra cotta lamp of the type that was also used by the Israelites. These lamps, with a long nozzle and groove for the overflow of oil, date from the end of the fourth century A.D. The figured disc in the center was usually ornamented with a scene from the Bible such as the Three Hebrews in the Furnace, the Sacrifice of Abraham, Jonah and the Whale, the Raising of Lazarus, or Christ Carrying the Cross. The scene was surrounded by a border of conventional ornament. Other lamps have a center ornament of a symbol, such as the cross, fish, or Good Shepherd. These were the little lamps that the Hebrews and other ancient peoples were accustomed to burning overnight in their chambers, often incorrectly translated "candles" in the Bible. Or look, if you will, at a little leaden oil flask with a scene of the Adoration of the Magi or at the souvenir water bottles that were sold to pilgrims to Palestine in the sixth century. The small minor arts of the early Christian and Byzantine periods are considered so valuable that the nucleus of the collection of Christian art at Dumbarton Oaks is given over to the jewelry, ivory, silver, metalwork, and textiles of religious significance.

By concentrating our emphasis on the Christian art of any one period or any one medium, we reduce God to too small dimensions. We need to remember that God reveals Himself in diverse ways, in many languages, many mediums, and in many art forms. If we read the story of the Christian Church together with the story of art down through the ages from the early beginnings of Christianity, a wide panorama of Biblical history comes alive before our eyes and takes us to hitherto unexplored regions of Christian understanding and aesthetic experience. There are richness and variety of styles in Christian art. Beginning with the Greek influence in the catacombs, the different great styles of the Byzantine, Romanesque, Gothic, Renaissance, and Baroque were followed by the lesser styles of the eighteenth and later centuries—classicism, romanticism, naturalism, impressionism, expressionism, cubism, surrealism, and the contemporary abstract style. Each style revealed something about its age and the men that lived in it. Christian art tells us much about man's spiritual life. It reveals his conception of the origin of the world and of human life. It tells us of his thoughts about death and the life beyond, and gives an insight into man's spiritual life and reveals his hopes, fears, virtues, and joys. It expresses his ideas of good and of evil and explores the social relationships of man to man.

In the past the Church employed the artist and craftsman with various purposes in mind. From the standpoint of the Church, art has a twofold function. Fine art, such as painting and sculpture, is used to proclaim the Gospel and to teach the stories of the Bible. The religious and aesthetic feelings of the artist are conveyed to the people. At first art was used to teach the doctrines and dogma of the Church. The Bible texts were closely followed, and no one thought of the artist as being divinely inspired. Instead, the artist was used by the Church, and was willing to follow the rules and instructions of the Church as to the choice and composition of subject matter. Art depicts not only the Bible stories but also the constant evolution of the Christian Faith from the time of the Apostles through the various edicts of the Church councils to the present day. The Church used the scenes of the Annunciation, the Last Supper, and the scenes of the Passion for the teaching of certain dogmas. Scenes that represent the three persons, Father, Son, and Holy Ghost, teach the doctrine of the Trinity: God is one tripersonal God. The scenes of the Transfiguration of Christ teach the doctrine of Transubstantiation; the Annunciation, Nativity, and Madonna and Child proclaim the doctrine of the Incarnation; while the doctrine of the Atonement is taught through the divinely appointed sacrifices of the Old Testament, culminating in the New Testament teaching that these were typical of the sacrifice Christ made of Himself by means of the Cross. Thus the Crucifixion becomes the subject of the doctrine of the Atonement.

Art can also, by means of architecture and its allied arts such as mosaic and stained glass, determine the mood of the house of worship, and even reflect the theology of the people and echo the liturgy of the service. The setting affects the devotional atmosphere of the church, particularly before the service begins. Self-forgetfulness and the impulse to adore are not called forth by ugliness. Private prayer can dispense with the arts; public prayer cannot. If we eliminate the objects of art that the Roman Catholic Church provides for the wandering mind, we must substitute beauty of proportion and color, and symbols that represent eternal values in new forms. Color is valuable as an adjunct to feeling. Not only does the tonal character of an interior influence people, but proportions such as symmetry can be an aid to worship, and the infinity of space can help us to escape to higher spheres of thought. Breadth expresses the intellectual concept, and height and length can aid in the expression of spiritual concepts. Art can also be used to decorate and enhance the various structures of worship, such as the altar, the pulpit, the lectern, and the articles of liturgical or ceremonial usage.

When is the content of a work of art Christian? When art expresses the spiritual aspects of the Christian Faith, it is Christian. What are some of the characteristics of Christianity that can be expressed in art? One aspect of the religious experience is that it calls forth emotions of awe and reverence and exaltation. These characteristics were most evident in the early Church and were expressed in early Christian and Byzantine art. In the Middle Ages contrition and conversion were important characteristics of the Faith, and these are also characteristics depicted in the subject matter of the art of the period. Later, in the seventeenth and eighteenth centuries, the Church put emphasis on confession and forgiveness, petition, veneration, and devotion, and these characteristics can be found in the paintings and sculpture of the period.

"Christian Art is the interpretation of beauty in life under the light of the Incarnation" (Hastings' *Dictionary of Christ and the Gospels,* Vol. I, Art.). In the Incarnation Christ becomes the bridge between the seen and the unseen and the justification and sanctification of all that is human. Thus, like the Incarnation itself, Christian art embodies the twofold conception of the spiritual destiny of the visible and of a spiritual revolution through the visible. The central fact of the Christian Faith gives a solid unity of both truths, and the office of art is to present the truth of things under the aspect of beauty. Thus the Christian artist is a teacher. His art is ministerial; it does not reflect as a mirror, but reveals and prophesies, and divine Love is his guide. There are some aspects of the Incarnation that art can reveal and that cannot be conveyed by words or symbols. Through the Madonna and Child, art helped man to realize that God who made heaven and earth also came into the world as the Child of a human mother. In the Middle Ages Christ's manhood was realized through art. The Bible scenes presented as everyday life make us feel the greatness of small things and the combination of majesty and human friendliness, the nearness yet the farness of Christ the King and yet the brother. But art has also given us the terror and sufferings of religion, and at times has taken from some scenes their awe and solemnity, and has given us pity instead of reverence. Sometimes a lack of spiritual imagination on the part of the artist has robbed us of the beauty of the simple Gospel words.

Christianity is too complex to be expressed in any single work of art, but the artist can interpret some aspect of Christian experience and express it in terms of one or more specific events, persons, or doctrines in the Christian tradition. Such Christian virtues as faith, hope, charity, purity, temperance, truth, wisdom, love, brotherly affection, humility, modesty, steadfastness, and vigilance are all worthy of expression in Christian art.

The human and tender aspects of the Gospels, the scenes of

the ministry of Christ, His gentleness and compassion, and the healing of the sick have possibilities of enlargement in art. The humanity of Christ, as shown in the parables and in His interest in nature, in the beauty of the lilies, His walking through the fields of grain, His pleasure in the garden in the cool of the evening, and His interest in everyday life have been overlooked by most artists in the past, although the Good Samaritan and the Story of Lazarus were favorite subjects with Protestant artists of the Reformation. These ethical and spiritual subjects have more appeal today than the miraculous and supernatural. Today's Christian art should also give dignity to work, produce fellowship, and teach us to love our neighbor as ourself. Artists must express the majesty of righteousness and the purity of truth as well as the glory of God on High.

The more significant the event or subject, the more profound will be the revelation of Christianity. Such a subject as the Crucifixion is more significant than the story of the Good Samaritan, but significant subject matter alone does not make great religious art. The spiritual quality is expressed when the artist conceives his subject with honesty and true feeling. All truly religious art makes visible the invisible, depicts the spiritual, and opens up the depth in the human soul.

The Christian qualities in art should be related to man and to the meaning of life. A Christian painting should be uplifting; no matter how unpleasant the subject matter, it should possess content that is uplifting and expressive of faith and hope. Abstract art also has its place in the expression of the Christian Faith. It can give us the beauty of line, rhythm, and color. Abstract art can express calm and peace, space, and the abstract beauty of color. It can express exaltation and joy, and even the beauty of holiness, which is a beauty of rhythm, repetition, and sound, such as was so profoundly embodied by Bach in the music of his B Minor Mass, one of the noblest outpourings of the Christian religious experience.

Art can express Christianity by means of symbols or by representation of scenes or historic episodes. Much religious art uses symbolic meanings that are unfamiliar to the average person. To get the whole religious meaning or significance, historical and iconographic information, as well as a knowledge of symbolism, are necessary. As Christians we understand the representations of the Crucifixion by such artists as Dürer or Tintoretto or Rubens which present the historical and dramatic scene, but the early representations of the Crucifixion, with their symbols of the sun and moon, skull and bones, and blood from the wounds being caught in a chalice seem strange to us, and need interpretation. On the other hand, Millet in his "The Angelus" interprets the simplicity of religious worship by means of sentimental symbols that we understand—bowed heads, hands folded in prayer, and a church spire in the distance.

The treatment of the subject matter of Christian art is divided into two classes: devotional and historical. Devotional pictures portray sacred personages alone or in groups as objects of veneration. The Virgin and Child alone or grouped with saints is a devotional subject, as is the Crucifixion with Christ alone on the Cross or with the Virgin and St. John. Representations of divine personages, as in "The Trinity" of Masaccio and pictures of Paradise or of the Coronation of the Virgin or of the Last Judgment, are devotional in purpose. Later devotional subjects include the Immaculate Conception, the Rosary, the Vision of St. Teresa, and Stations of the Cross.

When an incident or action is represented with sacred subject matter, the representation is historical. Stories of the Old Testament and incidents and miracles of the New Testament are usually treated historically. However, such subjects as the Last Supper and the Crucifixion may either tell a story or be so composed as to represent a symbol of redemption. When the Last Supper represents the scene of the institution of the Eucharist, it is devotional and symbolical; when it depicts the moment when Christ says, "One of you shall betray me," it represents a historical event. The Crucifixions showing Christ on the Cross with the sun and moon on either side and the chalice and Adam's skull at the foot of the cross are devotional and symbolical, while the scene with the crowds of soldiers, horsemen, and the two thieves becomes a historical representation. Flemish artists painted subjects such as the Annunciation as devotional pictures with mystical and symbolical meaning. The greatest of all mystical and symbolical scenes is van Eyck's "Adoration of the Lamb." Each figure is presented with symbolical meaning and arranged according to ecclesiastical code.

Early Christian artists depended on attitude and gesture to express feelings, since they did not have the skill to express emotion in any other way. In addition, many mediums of early art, such as ivory carvings and enamels, were too small in scale for detail.

The technique of mosaic did not allow detail, and the position of mosaics and frescoes high on the wall or in the apse or dome required simplicity of design in order to be seen. Sculpture has always relied on attitude and gesture to express inner emotional feeling, since strong emotion shown in facial expression destroys the monumental quality of sculpture. By means of posture and gesture, the sculptor can tell the story plainly, without the dramatic vehemence of surface detail.

The figure of the orant, or woman in prayer, in the art of the catacombs, in early ivory carvings, and in mosaics illustrates the ancient custom of saying prayers with hands parted and uplifted to shoulder height. This attitude emulates the position of Christ on the Cross and is an important gesture of the priest in the Mass of such liturgical Churches as the Roman Catholic, Episcopalian, and Lutheran. The hands are clasped in prayer or joined before the breast with palms together to express reverence, and this gesture is also given to the angels. Christ is depicted with clasped hands in the Baptism and also in most representations of the Agony in the Garden. The Virgin clasps her hands together when she kneels in adoration before the Christ Child, and the figure of a donor is usually shown kneeling with hands clasped in adoration. In the Mass joined hands are placed on the altar to express humility.

The gestures of the angel and the Virgin in the Annunciation are also closely related to the gestures of the Mass. The angel genuflects in reverence, and the right hand is sometimes held in the position of blessing or the sign of the cross with thumb and two fingers extended or, again in the early form, with the thumb and one finger. The Virgin is usually represented with eyes lowered and one hand to her breast or hands crossed on the breast in humility. Hands are covered to express reverence at certain places in the Mass, and we also see them covered with the same idea of reverence in the Ravenna mosaics and in certain paintings. Every gesture of the Mass is made with simplicity, solemnity, and restraint in order to express the utmost reverence and dignity. By emulating these gestures, artists produce a mood of quiet and worship that is deepened by the symbolism underlying each gesture and that adds to the religious interpretation of the scenes. Thus physical attitudes point to spiritual attitudes.

Many works of art with religious subject matter, such as "Joachim and Anna" or "Abraham Dismissing Hagar" by Rembrandt, which expresses the human pathos of the moment of parting, have a social appeal. Other religious pictures illustrate theological doctrines and may have great historical significance, but although their subject matter is religious they may have no emotional appeal and little religious expressiveness. Examples of such pictures are "The Dispute of the Sacrament" by Raphael and "The Dispute of St. Catherine" by Pinturicchio.

Many Madonnas of the old masters are not pictures with any deep religious feeling; they are merely pretty women holding children. Such a picture is Raphael's well-known "Madonna of the Chair." Filippo Lippi's "Virgin Adoring the Child" is a beautiful picture, but it is full of the love of the world. To be sure, there are the symbols of the Dove, the hand of God, and the golden rays descending upon the Child, but the artist's chief interest was in the beauty of the landscape and the sentimental aspects of the scene. In comparison, one cannot look at an early Madonna of Giovanni Bellini without a feeling of awe and reverence. The paintings of Fra Angelico also reveal the spiritual aspects of his subjects, and such a picture as "The Annunciation" expresses simplicity and heavenly glory. Only when the artist has the power to interpret the Christian content of the scene has it real religious significance.

Specifically, Christian art is the story of the Bible in art. From the beginnings of creation as told in Genesis through the books of the Prophets, Judges, and Kings, to the Birth of Christ, His Passion and Death, art reveals the scenes: sometimes in stark simplicity, with glowing fervor of expression, or in meticulous detail. We see Adam and Eve and the Tree of Life in the stone sculpture of the early sarcophagi or on the columns of a Gothic cathedral, or painted with minute detail by the German or Flemish painters. Noah, Daniel, and Moses were favorite subjects in early Christian art, and the Apostles stand in stately rows in Church sculpture and mosaics.

But the figure of Christ is the zenith and most profound expression of Christian Church art. The basic theme of Christian art illustrates the Faith of the Church as centered in Christ. Whatever the story or whatever the scene, the motif behind it all is to interpret the Faith and to illustrate each incident of Biblical history in the light of its meaning in connection with the coming of Christ. Thus Christ is always the underlying eidolon. Although Christian art is rooted in history, the sacramental rather than the historical is the province of the sacred artist. Art was first regulated according to a set plan that followed the requirements of the Church dogma and the interpretations of the clergy. In the history of Christian art as seen through the ages, we look for the art that implies faith and reverence. The greatest periods from the standpoint of the Church are therefore those in which the divine theme is the most important expression, rather than the technical excellence of the work of art, although good workmanship and integrity are also to be desired. However, the primitive efforts of early art often convey a deeper spirituality and reverence than the works of the greatest masters of the Renaissance.

The paintings of the Crucifixion that confine the scene to Christ on the Cross and the figures of Mary and John center our attention upon Christ and tell the story with clearness and simplicity. In more complex scenes of the Crucifixion our attention is often distracted by the faces of the mob or the landscape. We may admire the beauty of the scene and the technique of the artist, but our attention will be divided between these features and the content of the picture. Even the picture that includes the two thieves on their crosses loses some of its dramatic quality and its direct statement. Rembrandt's "The Supper at Emmaus" is an example of an artist's great skill controlled and concentrated on the impelling expression of his theme. Only a great artist, primitive or sophisticated, can stimulate the aesthetic experience and at the same time create religious feeling.

The Church first of all made use of art to teach. The early pre-Constantine art was crude and simple. But ornaments such as hunting scenes were used as early as the sixth century, and art soon outgrew its primitive forms and could be used to adorn the Faith and to refresh the perception of truths already known. Yet as far as art progressed technically and in the realm of the aesthetic, it added few new religious subjects to the repertory of the artist. From simple and nameless artists have descended the scriptural types and traditions that constitute the iconography or subject matter of Christian art. The early art was suited to the subject, and scenes are portrayed with reverence and piety. Symbols such as the nimbus, aureole, or glory are used to point out our Lord and thus give a divinity to even the rudest representations of Christ.

The sacramental character of Christian iconography demands

a certain economy of expression. At first the mystery was told by the use of symbolism, and the economy and restraint enabled the artist to communicate much by leaving much unsaid and to express truths that would require many words. Artists at first portrayed God by the symbol of the right hand emerging from a cloud. The hand is sometimes closed, but more often open and raised in the form of a blessing. It is a hand that expresses the thought and will of God, and the motion or gesture is one of assistance, commandment, benediction, or protection. The hand of God is seen in such scenes as the Offering of Cain and Abel. With His hand God orders Noah to build the Ark. The hand of God intervenes in the sacrifice of Isaac, the giving of the tablets of the Law to Moses, and other scenes in the Old Testament. It is rarely seen in the iconography of the New Testament, but emerges from the clouds to bless Jesus at His Baptism, and to console Him in the Agony of the Garden.

Sometimes two hands are seen. The hands are often invested with a nimbus in the form of a circle, the symbol of eternity and the geometrical symbol of God. The hand of God is sometimes seen holding a crown or an evergreen wreath over the head of Christ in a Crucifixion scene. Although the hand is the most frequently used symbol of God, in the Renaissance the eye with rays of light became the symbol of God and when set within a triangle stood for the Triune God or the Trinity. While early artists obeyed the second commandment and avoided pictorial representations of God, gradually the feeling of sacrilege was overcome and the head, then the bust, and finally the whole figure of God was shown. In wall paintings of the Creation at the Cathedral of Monreale the bust of the Father with the head set in the eternal circle and the hands outstretched is shown together with the dove and light rays in a symbolic scene, "The Spirit Moving on the Face of Waters." In both the "Creation of Angels and Light" and "God Resting on the Seventh Day," the figure of God is shown sitting on the symbolic circle or sphere. God is represented as the Ancient of Days in a white vestment with a white beard and long white hair sitting in the clouds on a throne of glory in early Byzantine art, and this became the typical Renaissance representation. Often there is a triangular halo, and God may hold a globe or book or architect's square or, later through the influence of Rome, He may be clad in papal dress with a papal tiara. The Creator is pictured full length with beard in the Creation series on the façade of the

Cathedral at Orvieto. In the Sistine Chapel Michelangelo pictures God as a Jove-like personage, and this likeness is followed by Raphael in his "Creation of Light." This image of God has persisted in art down to the present day, although there is no Biblical description that allows for this representation. Today a symbol is preferred. It need not, however, be the old symbol, but needs only the abstract qualities of awe, mystery, majesty, and grandeur and a divineness that sets God apart from other figures.

Christians also at first represented Christ by symbol alone, the fish being one of the most important. The Greek letters of the word "fish" are the initial letters of the words "Jesus Christ, God's Son, Savior." In this sense the fish symbol was used in early Christian art. However, the lamb as a symbol of Christ is one of the favorite and most often used. There are many types of the lamb symbol. The Good Shepherd carrying the lamb is seen in the catacombs. The lamb in the Crucifixion scene is sometimes substituted for the body of Christ on the Cross, but more often is lying at the foot of the Cross with blood from wounds flowing into a chalice. The lamb of the Resurrection carries a banner, while the mystical lamb of the Apocalypse stands with the four streams of Paradise, or is shown lying on a throne resting on a book among the seven candlesticks. Without book or candlesticks the throne becomes an altar and the lamb the sacrifice of the Eucharist. The idea of the lamb as Christ was prevalent in early Christian art until A.D. 692, when the council "in Trullo" ordered "that in the stead of the ancient Lamb, Jesus Christ our Lord shall be shown henceforth in his human form." However, the symbol of the Agnus Dei continued to be used, but the symbol was limited to the familiar one of a lamb holding a cross.

The representations of Christ in Majesty as Pantocrator are human in form yet symbolic in meaning. In the Byzantine churches this large figure with head enclosed in a crossed nimbus and right hand raised, the left hand clasping an open book, occupies the space in the dome. These Old Testament representations of our Lord are all of a moral or symbolic appearance. The New Testament pictures of Christ seek to represent Him in natural human form.

Since there are no descriptions in the Bible of what Christ looked like, but only of what qualities of character He had and what He did, each race and each artist sought to represent its or his ideal. Beginning with the classic beardless youth of Roman art, we then have the Byzantine representation with beard and parted hair. The Syriac triangular effect of hair and beard also influenced the portraits of Christ, while early Anglo-Saxon portraits are abstract in appearance. To the extent that the artist represents Christ in the great scenes of His life with an understanding of the religious significance of the scene, and is able to express the divine qualities in such a way that they glorify His features, that portrait is successful.

The artists of the fifteenth century sought to represent Christ as He walked among men. Art allows us to meet an inner, intimate Christ, not historical or theological. Each artist gives his own interpretation, and thus we have infinite diversity: the benign, forgiving Christ of Fra Angelico, the judging, the suffering, and the triumphant Christ. The Christ of Giotto and the Sienese primitives expresses human pity and mildness. Dürer and Grünewald show Christ tortured by conflict and doubt; van Eyck paints a sovereign judge; and the Christ of Mantegna is burdened with dereliction. Bosch paints the Ecce Homo of misery; the Christ of El Greco reflects violent and distressed Spain; and the Christ of Rouault is the Crucified One. In contrast, Tintoretto's and Tiepolo's Christ reflects the dazzling, sensuous Italy of their time, and Rubens' Christ is visionary, while later, nineteenth century interpretations are mawkish and have the varnish of conformity. Beginning with the human, less spiritual, less holy portraits, the profound conception of Christ finally evolves into that of a dreamy, weak man as He is seen portrayed by Holman Hunt, Heinrich Hofmann, and Bernhard Plockhorst.

The Holy Spirit in the form of a dove flying downward appears in representations of the Annunciation, at the Baptism of Christ, and as the symbol of the Holy Ghost in representations of the Trinity. In geometric symbolism the Trinity is represented by the triangle or three interlacing circles. A knowledge of these symbols of the Deity are necessary for our enjoyment of Christian art.

The language of the sign and symbol was in universal use in the Christian art of the past and was used to help reveal the mystical and spiritual meaning of religion. If we are fully to understand Christian art, especially of the Gothic and Renaissance periods, we must have a knowledge of this language of symbols. There were not only symbolic representations of the Deity; there were also symbols relating to the Apostles and saints, a geometrical symbolism relating to the cosmic world, a symbolism of animals and flowers, and a symbolism of numbers.

At first Christian art adhered closely to the text of the Bible, but as time went on the Bible stories were padded by later writers and their additions of myth and legend were incorporated into the religious art of later centuries. Superstition and doubt and religious dogma also changed the content of later Christian art. Stress on pain and suffering and an appeal to the emotions crept into Christian art through the teachings of different cults, religious orders, and inspired saints. Much of this art has an overpowering appeal to the feelings, and is accepted because of its sentimental quality. Certain other artists or schools of art took poetic license, departed from the exact text of the Bible, and added angels or other symbolic forms where the Bible does not mention them. Yet when such additions do not mar the truth, but add to the impressiveness of the scene, they are permissible, and since such themes are usually imaginative and decorative, the pictures are colorful and have aesthetic value.

Local color also creeps into the portrayal of scenes of Christian art. Thus the Nativity scene is sometimes set in a grotto and at other times in a stable, or the costumes may be those of a country or century different from those of the origin of the story. But these details need not interfere with the beauty or the spiritual significance of a work of art if they are secondary and subordinate to the Christian theme and if the artist is sincere and has the spiritual virility to give the proper over-all spiritual feeling.

Christian art is not really an isolated subject of importance only to Church people. Anyone interested in art eventually finds himself studying Christian art. Great museums and picture galleries must necessarily devote considerable space to Christian art because much of the finest art in the world has Christian subject matter. The colorful Byzantine mosaics, the beautiful stained glass of the Middle Ages, the great tapestries, the finest works of goldsmiths and silversmiths, and even the wall decorations of palaces of the Italian Renaissance have Christian subject matter. For the best-known artists in the Western world have at one time or another drawn inspiration for their works from the highest of all art sources, the spiritual, as revealed through the Christian Faith. Although Christianity supplied art with its loftiest themes and received in tribute some of art's greatest achievements, the artistic result owes its excellence for the most part to the artistic, not the religious, motif. Nevertheless art does not develop, but languishes when faith is lacking. Art attains its highest summits when in concert with the spiritual forces of religion, and especially when it mingles with it so closely that it is impossible to separate one from the other.

Art and the Christian religion have much in common. The beauties of sense and the mystery of God have a great similarity. The ultimate goal of the Christian Faith is some kind of vital union with the divine Being, and while the subject matter of art is life as it is, the function of art is to lift us beyond the realm of this world and to make life better. Artists have felt and expressed the unity between art and religion. "The true work of art is but a shadow of the divine perfection," is how Michelangelo expressed it. "If the doors of perception were cleansed everything would appear to man as it is, infinite," said William Blake in the eighteenth century.

When religious sentiment is at its height, it coincides with its greatest moment of energy, and something supernatural appears to rise from man to God. True art is also an expression of spiritual energy. It is this spiritual energy that creates an aesthetic experience that is important both to religion and to art, and here is the real value of art to religion, according to Croce—to stimulate the aesthetic experience that is an aid in worship. Worship itself is an art, but while art is not the aim of worship, if it is good worship an aesthetic activity is created. Good religion is not self-conscious. Because good religion forgets self in the greater sphere of humanity, so all good and efficient religious art should also forget self, and not be self-conscious. The aesthetic experience will not make religion flourish, but we can have no true religion without the aesthetic experience. Therefore it must be cultivated by all those who prepare the soil for the revelation of God today as in the past. Such moral works as the Gospels might pass unnoticed if they were not animated by artistic writing. And even the liturgy of the Roman Catholic Church would have less appeal without the Gregorian chant. Because of the beauty of the temple, the Byzantine church, and the Gothic cathedral, Christian religion became so much a part of the universal craving for beauty that the

Church was able to survive iconoclasticism and the morality of the Reformation.

In the story of Church art, each period needs a different understanding and a different point of view for the appreciation of its beauty. It is only through knowing a country and its people and understanding an age and the thought and philosophy of that particular epoch that we can come near to appreciating its art. In the great periods of Christian art, the art, religion, and the life of the people were all governed by the same compelling forces. Thus, the art was a true expression of the Christianity of the age. We must put ourselves in the atmosphere of the past as we try to understand what each artist and each age has to say, for art is of value only in the degree to which it speaks to us.

CHAPTER II

APPRECIATION OF CHURCH ART

A work of art has aesthetic value only as it becomes experience for a human being.

—JOHN DEWEY

Art should be interpreted in terms of appeal to the heart, mind, and soul. What art does for us and to us is more important than history or dates or the understanding of techniques. The work of art should communicate and we should experience. The highest level of artistic experience is participation in the creation of art, but this lies beyond the capacities of most men. The next highest experience is that which comes from understanding the origins, meanings, and emotions of creation. Without this understanding, experience belongs to the artist alone. But art appreciation and enjoyment is the privilege of all; it is not the property of the initiated few, for all can acquire the appreciation of art through education. By education I do not mean the study of the history, life, and times of the artists. This is not enough, although why, when, where, and how are clues to greater understanding.

Viewing great art of the past through visits to art museums and looking at reproductions in books will improve our experience and tastes to a certain extent. Indeed, the first step in getting to know art is to become familiar with it, for good taste is formed by seeing. Art is the prerogative of everyone with a pair of eyes. The seeing that leads to the appreciation of art is only the outgrowth of the activity of the eyes in everyday life. But we must open our eyes, look with fresh eyes, and venture to develop the fine art of seeing. If we see the best art and know why it is good, and also see the bad and understand why it is bad, our taste and appreciation are improved by this intelligent comparison and our enjoyment of art is increased. Art is concrete, and people's minds should not be confused with obscure aesthetic concepts and "arty" talk. We do not need to study aesthetics or psychology or delve deeply into the theory of art in order to enjoy and understand art, but we must have at least an inkling of the conditions of creation, its methods and objectives, if we want to broaden our enjoyment of art.

The first requisite for art enjoyment is a proper respect for and an honest effort to understand the artist's point of view. We tend to judge instead of trying to understand, and this erects a wall between us and the artist and the object of his creation. We have developed fixed likings of what we expect of art, and refuse to go beyond our personal experience. It is not necessary for us to give up what we like, but we can also expose ourselves to a wide range of works of art that will improve our taste and broaden our enjoyment. To appreciate art on its own terms the spectator must be humble and cultivate the proper attitude for receiving the message of a work of art. Enjoyment in art is an imaginary re-creation of the process through which the artist passes. Without this re-creation the object is not perceived as a work of art. In order to communicate with the artist, we must have a familiarity with the artist's language. Each artist has his own style, or handwriting, but he uses the universal language of art line, form, and color. We are able to communicate with artists of other countries and other ages because of this universal and enduring language of art in which line, mass, and color mean much the same today as they did centuries ago.

There are two channels in the approach to understanding and enjoying art. One is intuitive perception. This is the sensation or emotional effect of a work of art upon us when we first see it. Some people have this intuition more than others, and often persons wholly untrained in aesthetics have strong reactions toward the best in art.

We should start with the intuitive and spontaneous enjoyment of art, and analyze and interpret afterward. The artist also begins with feelings, and finds symbols to express them for our perception. If we come close to the work of art, and analyze it, we draw out our power of latent appreciation. This approach to art needs a key to translate the artist's language into our own. This is the intellectual approach to art appreciation, and it can be acquired by all who have the desire to learn. Real art appreciation depends upon orderly relationships, and is intellectual as well as emotional.

There is no one approach to art appreciation, but any path involves the knowledge of the language and grammar of art and the principles of art expression—balance, color, proportion, rhythm, variety, unity, harmony. The grammar of art begins with the three structural elements of art that are used in composing harmonies—line, dark and light, and color. Line is the boundary of a space. The arranging and grouping of interrelated lines in harmony with one another in a space produces the simplest form of beauty. This simple spacing of straight lines can be seen in a piece of furniture, such as a chest of drawers. American Indian art is composed of angular lines; Chinese landscape painting is made up of beautiful rhythmic curved lines; and interlacing patterns of lines are found in the pages of early illuminated manuscripts, such as the famous Book of Kells. A line gets form from its relation to other lines and by its use in connection with the other elements of color, mass, light, and space. Rembrandt and Michelangelo were masters of line drawing. In Rembrandt the merging of line, light, and color is so perfect and subtle that we do not differentiate between them, while in Michelangelo line and color are distinct but well related.

But lines also have psychological meanings that can be used by the artist to help express his emotions. Thus lines are not only vertical, horizontal, zigzag, and curved but also crooked, wavering, majestic, and calm. The horizontal line is the line of the horizon, and expresses calm and quiet. It is the dominant line of the Greek temple. The vertical line is uplifting and aspiring. It is the line of the Gothic cathedral and the repeated rhythmical line of a forest of trees. The broken zigzag is the line of jazz or broken harsh movement, while the curved line is the line of grace that characterizes the art of such artists as Botticelli.

Line creates the sense of structure and pattern that carries the core of the meaning of a work of art. Line also is descriptive, and gives character and suggests movement. Line can also express mood. It is the value of line to express mood that is important to the artist when portraying religious scenes. This spiritual quality of line was best understood by the Chinese Buddhist painters who produced the greatest religious paintings the world has ever known. But it was also understood by Christian artists of the West such as Botticelli, who used the curved line, and other Renaissance painters who composed circular compositions within the circle, and by the Gothic sculptors and El Greco, who used the vertical line to express aspirations of the soul.

Dark and light, or the massing of dark and light spaces in harmonious relations, is the second structural element of space art. This is not the same as light and shadow in nature; it is the artist's own creative way of massing light and dark. There may be beauty of dark and light without subject matter, as seen in geometric patterns of marble mosaic pavements. In nature a dark tree may make a harmony against a light sky. Coptic textiles and Greek vase painting are other examples of fine dark and light spacing. In painting, Whistler, Daumier, and Ryder come to mind as artists who achieve their effect mainly with a fine balance of dark and light tones. The light and dark masses create expressive forms and patterns in a work of art, and the character of volumes can be suggested through light and shade. Mass contrasted with space, such as a long figure against a simple background, as in Millet's "The Sower," gives volume and depth.

The third structural element of art is color. Because colors can produce quiet and restful effects and exciting and stimulating effects, the sensations produced by color can have much to do with the appeal of a work of art. Color acts like music, stimulating thought and memory. Color may be used in flat tone or its surface may have variety and richness, and by means of a multiplicity of tones and hues it can enhance its own surface and heighten the relations between other colors. A picture so composed becomes a symphony of color. The possibilities of variation and harmony of color were first explored by the Venetians, and the painting of Titian, Giorgione, and Tintoretto show this fluid use of color. Rubens and Renoir produced color with a glow and bloom that covers every inch of their canvases, and Rembrandt, although he used dark tones, suggests richness and variety of color. The most subtle use of color was understood by the Orientals. They use positive tints sparingly in large spaces of neutral tone with gray and black inks that heighten the color. The beauty of Oriental color is also due to the purity of the pigments. Variety of color and even of black ink is explained by the Japanese artist Hokusai: "There is the black which is old, and the black which is fresh, lustrous black and dull black, black in sunlight and black in shadow." The use of light with color produces atmosphere. This was the main theme of the impressionists such as Monet; but it was also used by the Venetians to produce a golden effect and by Corot in his silvery landscapes.

Color has a threefold nature: *hue*—red, blue, yellow; *value*—light to dark; light or dark red, light or dark blue, light or dark yellow; *intensity*—or bright to grayness; intense red, dull red. Color harmony depends upon the proper adjustment of this threefold nature of color; however, color appreciation is grasped by the emotional approach rather than by analysis. We learn and increase our enjoyment by seeing the best examples of color in enamels, Oriental rugs, Persian manuscripts, and Chinese art. Artists like Matisse broaden our enjoyment of color. Matisse took reds, oranges, and cerise and used them to produce harmonies that are new to the average person. El Greco used color and subject matter that was familiar, but by elongating his figures and giving emotional values to both color and line he produced something new. Giotto also used color to produce a mysterious effect. The religious character of a world transfigured is revealed by the limpid, sparkling glow of jewel-like, translucent colors in his paintings.

Ruskin expresses himself on the use of color in sacred art, and his words will help us to judge between the good and bad in works of Christian art: "In religious art . . . clearness, luminousness, and intensity of hue are essential to the right impression; and from the walls of the Arena Chapel in their rainbow play of brilliant harmonies, to the solemn purple tones of Perugino's fresco in the Albizzi Palace, I know not any great work of sacred art which is not as precious in colour as in all other qualities. . . . The pure white light and delicate hue of the idealist is the glory of heavenly rejoicing. Of all God's gifts to the sight of man colour is the holiest, the most divine, the most solemn. The more faithful and earnest the religion of the painter, the more pure and prevalent is the system of his colour. Where colour becomes a primal intention with a painter . . . it instantly elevates him and becomes the one sacred and saving element in his work. Surely as a painter is irreligious, thoughtless or obscene in disposition, so surely is his colouring cold, gloomy and valueless."

There are five principles of composition, or ways of using the elements of the language of line, dark and light, and color in order to create harmony. They are subordination, repetition, symmetry, opposition, and transition. *Subordination* is an important principle in all the fine arts. In order to have unity and order there must be subordination, which means that one line, mass, or color must be more dominant, and all others related to it. This can be done by grouping together or by radiation as in a rosette. Illustrations of subordination in nature are a tree with its branches, a flower, such as a daisy, with its center, and a range of mountains with its one tall mountain peak. *Repetition* produces beauty by repeated use of the same lines in rhythmical order. The intervals may be equal, as in a frieze or border, or unequal, as in a landscape. Repetition must be rhythmically spaced in order to create harmony. This is illustrated by the difference between walking and marching. *Opposition* is created when two lines meet. It is a simple and severe harmony seen in landscape when vertical lines (trees, a church steeple, a mast of a ship) cut the horizon. *Transition* is made by introducing a third line, or tone or color, to tie two abrupt elements together. Its simplest line form is a bracket. *Symmetry* is the simplest way to create order and balance. The two sides of a vase are symmetrical; the human body is symmetrical; a design of a tree with two birds, one on either side of the trunk, is symmetrical. These elements of design are not of themselves magical recipes for good art, but are dependent upon proportion and good spacing. All the elements of design are put together by means of composition.

A great deal of our enjoyment of art comes from composition. Composition is the arrangement, spacing, proportioning, and distribution of line, dark and light mass, and color of figures or objects. There may be one or many points of interest in a work of art, but they must be unified and brought together in a harmonious relationship so that our eyes see them in unison. The composition should also focus on the central point of interest. Compositions can be built up on a line structure of vertical, horizontal, or diagonal lines. A vertical pattern is the simplest, and single figures or a group of figures standing, as Rodin's "St. John the Baptist," are based on the vertical line structure. Leonardo da Vinci's "The Last Supper" is an outstanding example of horizontal line composition. A curve or arch is often the dominant line of organization in a work of art. This dominant curve is the structure used by Rembrandt for many of his pictures. The ultimate form of the curved line is the circle, which also serves as structure for painting and sculpture. The circle suggests unity and completeness. Many of Botticelli's Madonnas are constructed on a spherical composition, and Della Robbia and Michelangelo used the circle for compositions of Madonnas in plastic relief. The diagonal line was used structurally by Tintoretto, and a scheme of spirals is the structural basis of many pictures by Rubens. But the spiral composition is more simply illustrated by sculpture, since spirals are three-dimensional. Giovanni da Bologna's well-known bronze "Mercury" is based on a graceful spiral line.

There are several types of mass composition. The simplest form is that of a triangle with a central mass or figure and balancing figures at the right and left. This type of composition is seen in most of Raphael's Madonnas, in certain Crucifixions, such as Perugino's "Crucifixion with Saints," and in the tympanums over the doorways of Romanesque and Gothic church portals. The central figure is usually the one of greatest interest and importance, and the other figures are tied together in a relationship with the central figure. Much free-standing sculpture is also based on a triangle. The space composition of Renaissance painting used a structure of architectural forms, the circle, the triangle, or cone. Archways opening and revealing distant landscape give an open-air feeling of space. The greatest space composition in Christian painting is seen in the work of Perugino and Raphael. It is composition in three dimensions that has the effect of taking us out of ourselves and giving us an exalted feeling of identity with the universe. This sort of art is closely allied to religion and can thus aid in communicating religious concepts. Without this spaciousness much of the glory and dignity of Raphael's great religious paintings would fade. Structure enables the artist to lift his expression above the commonplace and give it a universal meaning.

Paintings of the highest art value are composed with color as well as with line and form, and the color structure, together with the sequence of line and mass, builds and binds the elements of the picture together. The emotional, mystic, and psychological qualities of color can be used by the Christian artist as an aid to expressing spiritual and Christian values and as a stimulus to devotion and contrition. Much of the mystic and otherworldly atmosphere in the paintings of van Eyck and Perugino is due to their use of quiet blues and greens. Van Eyck also uses color to give the effect of space and order, with the warm colors and high intensities in the foreground and the cool, soft, low-intensity tones in the backgrounds. Giotto's tactile sense is due to gradation of color. Color is also used symbolically—the Virgin is given a blue robe for purity, and white, the color nearest light, was used for garments in such scenes as the Assumption, the Transfiguration, and the Resurrection. Gold as related to the sun and light also expressed infinity, and, together with purple or red, majesty. The blacks and browns are earthly colors, and red and black are used in Purgatory and Hell.

Finally, all organization and composition in a work of art is for the purpose of conveying content. Artistic content is not the beauty or aesthetic quality of the composition's form or medium, nor is it the artistic quality of the subject matter. The chief content of a work of art consists in the artist's interpretation of certain universals. This universal content of a work of art may be perceptual—something we can see, such as a tree or a color—or it may be spiritual—social, religious, or introspective. The deeper and more complex the expressed content of a work of art, the more significant is the work of art. The great artist is never satisfied to be a mere creator of beauty, but always strives to probe the truth beneath the surface and to express his interpretation of a wider reality and a richer experience. Yet no work of art can tell the whole story, and only certain aspects of the chosen universals can be emphasized by the subject matter. Great art must have something more than formal beauty, for art is not perfection of design and composition or finesse of technique. There is a difference between flawlessness and sublimity. Great art shows the universal shining through the particular. To be great, art must have this universal content. The art that moves us most is that which ennobles life and expresses a profound experience. The subject matter alone does not constitute the greatness of art or its character as Christian or religious art. It is the artistic interpretation of man's most poignant social or religious experience to which we ascribe greatness, and the interpretation is great to the extent that the artist has depth of imagination and intensity of emotional response that are necessary for breadth of outlook and to probe the ultimate reality beneath the visual surface of things. Every real work of art is numinous: it fills the observer with fear and joy.

CHAPTER III

EARLY CHRISTIAN ART

1. The Beginnings: Sepulchral Art

In the beginning was the Word, and the Word was with God, and the Word was God.

—John 1:1

Christian art developed simultaneously in many parts of the ancient world and was an expression of the art of diverse peoples. Although early Christian art varied with each race and environment, there was an over-all unity, and it is important that early Christian art be envisioned as a whole, for although the forms and expressions differ, the themes, iconographic form and feeling expressed were the same. Christian art had a different meaning and purpose and sought new values. It disregarded three-dimensional space and substituted infinite space. A spiritual or metaphysical interpretation was desired rather than natural appearance, and this was accomplished by the use of symbols that were coordinated into set schemes of thought expressing the fervor and simplicity of the early Christian Faith.

All the regions of the nearer East where Christianity first developed had something to give, and all elements were bound together in a continuity. Each region left its own legacy that was taken over and adapted by the Church. Thus Christian art was not suddenly created, but in each country it used the pagan art already existing and Christianized its forms so that they could be employed in the service of the Christian Faith. Although the initial influences were many, two important ones stand out: the Classic from Greece and the Oriental from the Near and Far East. The infiltration of the characteristics of these two influences can be traced in Christian art from the beginnings down through the centuries.

Whether Christian art first began in the catacombs of Rome, in Palestine, in Dura, in Asia Minor, or in Alexandria, Egypt, is not important for us here. We leave that to the experts. What is of interest is that each locale bequeathed its native influence and that it was a combination of these influences that created the definite style and format of Christian art. The first Classic influence on Christian art was the picturesque style that predominated in both Italy and in Alexandria in the illustrated books of the Old Testament such as the Rotulus of Joshua. However, the Italian interpretation of the style was narrative, factual, and prosaic, which was important in teaching the stories of the Bible and the dogma of the Church, whereas the picturesque art of Alexandria was more poetic, and included such Egyptian motifs as animals and ornamental vines. But the art expression of both Alexandria and Italy was built upon the foundations of Greek Classic art. The two styles mingled in the frescoes at Pompeii several centuries before the first Christian art. These lay frescoes in turn had an influence on all Christian art that came afterward. The custom of enclosing pictures in a framework, the still-life scenes, the architectural elements, the looped curtains, and the landscape panoramas are all seen to a small extent in the catacombs, but to a greater extent in mosaics, manuscript illustrations, and ivory carvings. Early Christian art in Italy and Alexandria is so dominated by Greek art that in many cases it is difficult to distinguish the early Christian art of this style from its pagan Greek model.

In Asia Minor and Syria an Oriental art style, forceful, vigorous, and emotional, exerted a different influence on early Christian art. This art was related to the modern expressive style of art today. In this type of art, the artist seeks to express the feeling and inner emotions of his subject. To do so, he often sacrifices beauty and even likeness. This early Christian expressive art is rigid and frontal. Heads of figures are often enlarged, and bodies are ill proportioned and squatty. Strong colors such as yellow ocher, sepia, gray-blue, and salmon-red are placed in sharp contrast. Early Christian expressionist sculpture is rough in surface finish. The well-known example of this style is the group of figures of the two tetrarchs in the southwest corner of St. Mark's at Venice. Paintings in the churches at Dura have an Eastern iconography of Christian art of this expressive style dating about the same time as the Roman catacombs. It is thought that the early churches

Constantine built in Constantinople in the fourth century but which have long since been destroyed were also decorated in this style. A wooden reliquary from this period is in the Vatican; it has scenes of the Nativity, the Baptism, the Crucifixion, the Marys at the tomb, and the Ascension, painted in the Eastern expressionist style. Of this same style are Syrian ivory carvings and the famous manuscript of the Gospels of Rabula; also, the work of Egyptian Christians or Copts as shown in their textiles, steles, or gravemarkers, and carved ivories, terra cotta lamps and ampullas and the frescoes in such monasteries as St. Simeon at Aswan have scenes painted in this style. In this art of the Egyptian Christians or Copts we see the Bible stories and such symbols as the Cross, the Chi Rho, the Alpha and Omega, the grape and vine, angels, birds, shells, and baskets of fruit mingled with pagan scenes of the chase, Venus, Leda, Hercules, bacchantes, and marine deities. And we question whether a figure of a man with a lyre is David or Orpheus. The typical Christian cross of the Copts is the Maltese cross, but we also see the pagan cross ansata of the Egyptians.

The second Classic influence that played an important part in the formation of early Christian art is what Morey calls "neo-Attic." This was a conservative Greek style that had developed several centuries before Christian art began. It was marked by excellent craftsmanship with fine modeling and sharp, well-defined outlines. It was academic and unemotional. It flourished in Antioch and other Greek cities of Syria, in Rome, and in Constantinople, and is seen especially in the imperial sarcophagi and in ivory carvings of Constantinople. The work is polished and has excellent technique. The Classic and Oriental influences merged together to be used later in the service of the Church. By a blending of elements from the Classic Greek and the emotional expressive Oriental, together with the many regional and national influences, the art of the early Christian Church was developed.

The evolution of early Christian art began in the catacombs. There were also catacombs in Naples, North Africa, and as far north in Europe as Cologne. However, the catacombs at Rome are the only ones that are in a state of preservation so that we can study their art. Furthermore, the Roman catacombs had particular distinction because of the tradition that Peter and Paul and other martyrs were buried there. Thus the catacombs became a place of religious reverence and devotion. The catacombs were cemeteries and not primarily places of worship, but they included chapels where Eucharistic services were sometimes held in memory of the dead. Bits of red-stained wineglasses used in these services were found embedded in the cement of tombs. In the ninth and tenth centuries A.D., the relics of the saints were removed and the catacombs were closed and forgotten until accidentally discovered by laborers in 1578. Although there were churches above ground that were in use at the time of the catacombs, they no longer exist, and the catacombs supply us with much of the available information about pre-Constantine Christian religion. Thus our story of early Christian art will begin with the sepulchral art of the catacombs.

In the crude paintings of the catacombs, we can see the influence of the fresco paintings of Pompeii in the formal framework of the ceilings and the use of still life. However, the paintings in the catacombs reflect the work and tastes of a different social order. The early Christians for the most part were poor and could not afford the best artists. More important was the fact that their interests and outlook were different. The art of the catacombs is more a language than an art, and less in the realm of art than in that of archaeology. However, it is important in the story of Church art because here, for the first time, the essential tendencies of Christian art are revealed.

At first the fresco painting in the catacombs was confined to names and inscriptions painted in red paint or scratched in the clay walls. The paintings included such well-known symbols as the Cross, the Alpha and Omega, and the Chi Rho; the anchor of hope; the fish, the Greek letters for which signify "Jesus Christ, God's Son, Savior"; the dove, symbol of heavenly bliss and peace; the palm denoting victory; the ship, symbol of the Church; and Christ in the form of the Good Shepherd. These symbols were all taken over from pagan Roman art but were used with Christian meaning. When artists first passed beyond simple inscriptions, decoration was added to make the tomb cheerful. Ornamental subjects included such cycles as the four seasons, which, though pagan, seemed relevant to the cycles of human life.

With the introduction of Old Testament subjects in about the third century, this art had already become subservient to the teachings of the Church. Theological ideas of this period are conveyed by pictures enabling the mind to recall the significance of the stories. The general theme of the art of the catacombs was resurrection or the hope of everlasting life, pardon, regeneration and deliverance from evil. The pictures teach the power of Christ to heal the sick and raise the dead. Such Bible stories as Noah, Jonah, Daniel and the Lions, Moses Smiting the Rock, the Three Hebrews in the Fiery Furnace, Abraham and Isaac, the Healing of the Paralytic, and the Raising of Lazarus are shown representing the theme of deliverance. Since these incidents are all found in early prayers of the Church, especially the "Deliver, O Lord" prayer still used in the Roman Catholic Church, it is thought that the frescoes may illustrate these prayers.

In such representations the brevity of the illustration reduces the subject almost to bare symbolism. The sacrament of the Lord's Supper is shown in the Miracle of the Loaves and Fishes. The multitude is represented by seven persons and there are seven baskets of loaves and two fish. Noah stands in an ark that is a mere box, Daniel stands between two lions, and the paralytic appears alone with his bed on his back. The sacrament of Baptism is also portrayed.

The paintings of the catacombs also give us our first Madonna. The figure of the orant, a woman with hands outstretched as in prayer, which was later used so much in early Christian art, is one of the most popular symbols of the catacomb frescoes. Although Christ is portrayed as the Good Shepherd, there is at first no attempt at individual portraiture; the figure is taken over from the Greek-Roman representations of Hermes, a youth with short, curly hair. However, a bust of Christ, dating from the fifth or sixth century, shows Him with long hair, a beard, and with one hand raised in blessing, the other holding a book, a representation that is to be repeated again and again in the cycles of Christian art. Decorative details consist of borders of doves and baskets of fruits. These have been interpreted as symbolizing the human soul feeding on the fruits of Paradise. In all these pictures are the germ and pith of the later cycles of Christian art.

Although such bold and courageous Christians as Stephen, Peter, Paul, Timothy, and Andrew braved arrest, imprisonment, chains, and death, the average early Christian worshiped in an "upper room," held his Eucharistic service for the dead in the catacombs, and clothed his language and art in symbols with pagan as well as Christian meanings. Such symbols did not invite arrest or persecution, while representations of Christ and His Crucifixion would have invited persecution. Thus, to avoid conflict with Roman authorities they were seldom used.

The art of the early Christian religion was joyous. We see none of the sufferings of our Lord—no mockings, no flagellations, no crucifixions—but not because the life of the early Christian was without these sufferings, for quite the contrary was true. However, the art of Rome of which the early Christians availed themselves had been developed by the Greeks, a race whose gods had beauty, dignity, youth, and repose. The treatment of early Christian subjects reflects these qualities.

While Roman Christians were painting symbols on the walls of the catacombs, a similar iconography of Christian fresco painting was developing in Dura and in the monasteries and convents of Africa. Recent excavations at Dura on the Euphrates River have brought to light a church and a synagogue dating back to the third century A.D. The baptistery of the church and the synagogue are painted with frescoes of Bible scenes. By the font of the baptistery of the church is a picture of the Good Shepherd. On the wall is painted Christ Healing the Paralytic, and the Three Women at the Holy Sepulcher. The side walls of the synagogue are painted with Old Testament scenes.

Christian paintings in Egypt begin with the frescoes of the catacomb of Karmuz at Alexandria and the chapels at Bagawat and Bawit. As in the Roman frescoes, we see the Multiplication of Loaves and Fishes and the story of Jonah, as well as a series of scenes of the departure of the Israelites from Egypt. All these paintings are crude illustrations that endeavor to tell a story but have very little art value. There is little organization of line or mass and no attempt at decorative spacing. Colors are harsh and are not used to create harmonies.

The themes of early Christian art of the Old Testament were also influenced by the Rotulus of Joshua, the first Greek version of the Old Testament that was produced in Alexandria and still exists in the Vatican Library. Its style relates to the columns of Trajan and Marcus Aurelius, but it also includes a landscape of mountains and groups of buildings that influenced the backgrounds of Byzantine mosaics and even the frescoes of later Italian artists.

When archaeologists opened the catacombs, they also found marble sarcophagi that had been used for the burial of persons of wealth. The largest collection of sarcophagi was found in Rome. Because sarcophagi were used for burial before the Christian era, some found were carved with pagan mythological scenes. Many others had the same scenes of Christian iconography as were painted on the catacomb walls. However, there was more picturesque detail in the carvings on the sarcophagi, and some have real aesthetic worth. Their heavy style and crowded compositions, as well as many details of their design, conform to the old conventions of Greek art. Although much of the subject matter is the same as in the catacomb frescoes, many new themes from the Bible are also to be seen. Noah, Daniel, Moses, Jonah, and the Good Shepherd are still found, but there are also Elijah, the Arrest of Peter, the Miracle of Cana, and the pagan scene of Ulysses and the Sirens. New Testament scenes predominate, including the Birth of Christ with the shepherds and the magi, the miracles, and the story of the Passion and the Resurrection. There are also many themes that have a close relationship with those used later in the decoration of the apses of the early churches. We see Christ seated on the throne among His disciples, Christ in Glory seated above the earth, or standing upon a mountain with a scroll in His hand, delivering the law, and Christ as judge. The empty throne with the cushion, cross, and book is the throne of Christ, and this is indicated by the dove above the throne. Many of our beautiful and decorative symbols such as the jeweled cross, the cross and wreath, and the Chi Rho in a wreath are also represented on these sarcophagi.

From the standpoint of design and workmanship, the sarcophagi vary. The subject matter is generally crowded into abbreviated episodes, and often it takes an outline guide to distinguish the different stories. There are several types of sarcophagi. The most common Roman type sarcophagus has its designs arranged in a frieze. In order to crowd more stories in, there may be a double frieze. Often the portrait busts of the persons buried in the sarcophagus are placed in a medallion or conch shell set in the center of the frieze. Another type of sarcophagus has its story episodes set in niches of Roman columns and arches.

From the standpoint of art certain sarcophagi are of particular interest. One of the most beautiful is the Good Shepherd Sarcophagus dating from the third century, now in the Lateran Museum in Rome. A beautiful network of vines and cherubs, birds, and baskets of fruit form the background for three figures of the Good Shepherd carrying the lamb about his shoulders. This design is related to that on the Chalice of Antioch in the Cloisters of the Metropolitan Museum in New York City, and is Eastern in origin.

Although the pursuit of the beautiful was not the chief interest of early Christian art, the figures of Christ and the Disciples on the Sarcophagus of Junius Bassus are Apollonic in conception and refined in workmanship. This sarcophagus is divided into two colonnades; each archway contains a different scene from the Bible. The most interesting panels are those containing the majestic figure of Christ enthroned above the earth, the decorative panels below of Adam and Eve with the serpent and Tree of Life, and the scene of the Entry into Jerusalem. This sarcophagus is now in the crypt of St. Peter's in Rome, Italy.

The Sarcophagus of Theodore, Bishop of Ravenna, is of still another type. On the rounded lid are carved two crosses and a Chi Rho each with attached alpha and omega and surrounded by wreaths. On the front is another Chi Rho monogram flanked by a pair of peacocks and decorative vines and grapes. Such sarcophagi reveal the rich beauty and symbolism of Christian art.

Until the third century A.D. Christian art consisted mainly of the childlike frescoes in the catacombs, illustrated Old Testament rolls, and the crowded Classical sculpture on the sarcophagi. Although it was a sepulchral art, it established the pattern of Christian iconography, declared two of Christianity's sacraments, and set the stylistic pattern of Christian art for centuries to come. In the next period of development, Christian art comes from underground and becomes monumental in scope.

2. Constantine: Triumphal Art

In the days of Pope Silvester, Constantine Augustus made the Lateran Basilica, the which he comely adorned.

Christianity and Christian art had a champion in the Emperor Constantine. Led by the vision of a fiery cross that he saw in the Roman sky, Constantine decided to sponsor the cause of the Christians, and at the same time consolidate his own empire. He took the monogram of Christ, Chi Rho, as his standard and set up his empire in the Eastern city of Byzantium, which he called Constantinople. In A.D. 313, with the Edict of Milan (called the Peace of the Church), Constantine gave toleration to Christians. A few years later he made Christianity the official state religion. Finally, in A.D. 325 Constantine presided at the Council of Nicaea, which sought to unite the Churches of the East and West, but is best remembered for giving us the Nicene Creed.

Having thus cemented the affairs of the Church and State, Constantine set up a program of church building that brought in a new era of Christian art and architecture. The Church art of Constantine is full of pomp and glory. It is monumental and imperial in scope. His imperial craze for splendor sought to eclipse the glory of Rome and Greece. Marble and porphyry columns from pagan temples were made to serve in the new churches. The finest artists were hired to decorate the churches with sculpture of gold, silver, and bronze, marble pavements and wall coverings, and colorful gold mosaics. These palatial church interiors spread as an imperial fashion to all parts of Constantine's empire—to Antioch, Rome, and Jerusalem.

In Constantinople the emperor set up a forum with columns of porphyry, and on the shaft of one column was cut the name of Constantine together with the cross he saw in the heavens and the inscription "Holy, Holy, Holy" in Greek letters. "By the fountains in the middle of the forum were figures in gilt bronze of the Good Shepherd and of Daniel with the lions; in the palace was a cross wrought in gold with many coloured precious stones" said Eusebius in *The Life of Constantine.* Socrates Scholasticus tells us that Constantine built two churches in Constantinople, "one he called Irene and the other The Apostles." The Church of the Holy Apostles was built near the forum, and Constantine was later buried in this church. In this church, which was in the form of a Roman mausoleum, cross-shaped with a dome, Constantine erected twelve marble columns to hold the dome. These columns represented the Twelve Apostles. Constantine also presented twelve marble columns to the original church of St. Peter's in Rome, where eight of them are still preserved in the balconies of St. Peter's. He also gave the Pope the palace and church of the Lateran.

Two of the most famous churches that Constantine founded were the Church of the Nativity at Bethlehem and the Church of the Holy Sepulcher in Jerusalem. Although little trace of the original churches is to be found today, we know from the writings of Eusebius that they had gilded ceilings, marble columns and pavements, and treasures of gold and silver.

In A.D. 326, when the excavations were being made for the churches in Jerusalem, Constantine's mother, Helena, visited the building sites and, going down into the diggings with the workmen, discovered the three crosses of Calvary. She sent part of the Cross of Christ, or the "True Cross," to Constantinople. "In S. Sophia is the Cross of the Lord which Helena the queen brought." Part remained in Jerusalem in the Church of the Holy Sepulcher. There is evidence that in the fifth and sixth centuries portions of the True Cross could be obtained in Constantinople, and fragments of the Cross are in reliquaries throughout the world. The relic of the Cross is often represented in the form of a double-armed cross, for the excavated Cross was recognized as the Cross of Christ because of this extra crosspiece, which held the inscription.

In order to understand and appreciate this era of Church art that is monumental and has primarily to do with Church architecture and decoration, we should know something about the form and appearance of the church building. Churches were built for Christian worship several centuries before Constantine. These dome-topped mausoleums and baptisteries, square or circular in shape, served as models for the majority of the churches Constantine built. The dome, pine cone, cosmic egg, melon, heavenly bowl—by whatever name it was called—was envisioned by the Syrians as a replica of the universe. The dome was also associated with the Syrian tent form, and we see representations of this tent form in early ceiling frescoes. "He hath established heaven as a vaulted chamber and stretched out as a tent to dwell in." On early coins the Ark is shown with a domical covering, like the ciborium over the altar. Roman tombs and martyries were dome-shaped; important people are represented as sitting or standing under a dome; and the earliest representations of the Last Supper show a sigma or dome-shaped table. Thus tradition and symbolism of the East and Biblical records established the monumental dome as an important feature of Church architecture, and it has remained so for many centuries.

The cruciform church also was popular in the time of Constantine, and the free-form shape with transepts and crowned with a dome celebrated the triumph of the Cross. An inscription by St. Ambrose in a church in Milan, Italy, reads: "This church is in the shape of a cross: the church is dedicated to Christ's triumphs and the sign of victory seals the place." Constantine built cruciform churches of two types. The first type showed a clear cross outline on the ground; the second had a Greek cross inscribed within a square and was only discernible from above. A celestial dome rose as a cabochon jewel from the center of the cross.

Another type of church structure, the basilica, was also used by Constantine. This type, the outgrowth of the Roman basilica, the Roman palace, and temples of pagan sects, was also discovered to have existed in the church at Dura as early as the 3rd century A.D. The façade was designed to attract people into the church. The entrance court was for the unbaptized, and the nave and side aisles were for the congregation. The basilica had an oblong rectangular plan with central nave, arcaded side aisles, a triumphal archway, and sometimes a transverse aisle inserted at right angles between the nave and a semicircular apse. The flat ceiling was constructed of wood. The form of the basilica was adapted to the demands of the Christian cult and the practical needs of the congregation. With its long central aisle and two side aisles divided by arches and pillars, it provided space for the congregation who stood in the side aisles. The doors were at the end of each aisle. There were no windows in the lower walls. The windows in the clerestory above admitted light and air, but permitted no outside view. The altar was placed in the apse. The early altar was small, but was given importance by the dome or ciborium that rose above it as a canopy and was supported by four columns resting on the pavement. Behind the altar was the cathedra, or bishop's chair. Through space this type of building suggested the infinite, and was thus a step toward the Christian expression of its spiritual content. This early church architectural plan has continued with variations down to the present day.

The architecture of the early Christian Church was based on symbolism and was a graphic way of conveying mystic ideas. Since the time of Diocletian the Romans had recognized the value of impressive architectural forms as a means of conveying ideas to strengthen popular beliefs. Royal processions were high-lighted by the construction of monumental gateways or triumphal arches. To show the heavenly authority of the divine sovereign, such cosmic architectural structures as the towered façade, dome, cupola, ciborium, *orbis,* and domed vestibule were used in palace architecture, and these celestial symbols were adapted by the Christian Church and are seen in Christian art and architecture from earliest times. The towered façade, a symbol of sacred dwelling used over Syrian temples, transformed the Roman or Byzantine church into a royal House of God. The monumental baldachin over the entrance to palace-churches in Constantinople became the narthex of the Christian church. The ruler entered the church through the arched "Royal Portal" between the "Towers of Heaven." In the narthex he was received with ceremonies under a rich brocaded canopy and then conducted to his seat in the domical apse above the narthex, which was reached by stairs that led to the towers. In Syria there were four towers over the church and stairs which the priest used to commune with the sun-god. In the fifth or sixth century these towers appear in Christian architecture along with the "Royal Door," and the church becomes the *Domus Dei.* The Christians also appropriated from palace tradition the ceremonies, insignia, regalia, acclamations, music, vestments, art, and decorations in order to present the Son of God in the impressive terms of a divine Imperator. Since palaces, temples, kings, and gods were related in the minds of the people as well as in the language of the Bible, this was a comprehensible means by which the spiritual import of Christian beliefs could be made apparent to a public accustomed to visualizing divinity in imperial terms. The writings of St. Germanos in the eighth century show how the Church sought to interpret the meaning of its architecture: "The Church is heaven upon earth, the place where God dwells and moves. It represents the Crucifixion, the Sepulcher, and the Resurrection of Christ." And in the thirteenth century Durandus writes, "The towers are preachers and prelates, Evangelists."

The frescoes and mosaics on the church walls enhanced this sense of religious mystery, wonder, awe, and enclosed space by creating a world apart—a world of spiritual realities invoked by the liturgy of the Church. The architectural background not only formed a setting for the decorations but also enveloped them as a cloak, and the grandeur of one enhanced the grandeur of the other, so that the effect was overwhelming. The words in the service of dedication of the Roman Catholic Church give the effect the church had upon the beholder: "Surely the Lord is in this place. How dreadful this place is; this is none other but the house of God, this is the gate of Heaven."

The architectural divisions of the early church were followed out in the scheme of painted and mosaic decoration. Thus the mysteries of the Faith and those things pertaining to the next world were placed in the dome of the apse, which represented the dome of heaven. There was the jeweled Cross triumphant, or Christ with the Apostles or Christ Pantocrator or the Good Shepherd with his sheep. A similar subject was placed on the wall above the triumphal arch that separated the apse and the nave of the church. On the walls of the nave were the episodes of the acts of God in history from the Old and New Testaments.

Although the churches that were built by Constantine in the East have been destroyed, there are a few fourth- and fifth-century churches in Rome with mosaics that follow this early sequence of church decoration. The earliest mosaics are those in the Lateran Baptistery and in the Church of Santa Costanza that was built by Constantine as a tomb. But the remains of these badly restored mosaics hardly give us a picture of what the rich decorations must have been or the grand scale of decoration of the Christian Church at this time. A sketch of the mosaic in the Lateran dome shows us a fantastic fishing scene with an intermingling of pagan and Christian symbols, and from descriptions in writings of the age we know that both fishing and hunting scenes were often used in early church decoration even before the time of Constantine.

The mosaics in the apse of Santa Pudenziana in Rome are a foretaste of the grandeur of mosaics to come. The theme in the apse is the Great Commission. Christ is seated on a throne in the midst of the disciples; He holds a scroll in one hand, while the right hand is raised. He is represented with long hair and a beard after the Eastern manner. Above and behind is a large gemmed cross against a background of clouds and the apocalyptic beasts. The space between is filled with scenes of the cities of Jerusalem and Bethlehem, representing the Holy City.

A series of panels on the walls of the Church of Santa Maria Maggiore are also of this early period. They include such scenes as the Hospitality of Abraham and Melchizedek presenting bread and wine to Abraham. These sacrificial scenes from the Old Testament are antetypes of the great sacrifice of Christ's body and blood reenacted in the Mass or Eucharistic feast. On the triumphal arch are scenes of the life of the Virgin.

The mosaics in the apse of Santi Cosma e Damiano depict the figure of Christ standing against a background of drifting flame-colored clouds. Below is a delightful frieze of sheep—one of the first of such processions of sheep—that march through early Church mosaics. The figure of Christ is represented with a mystical grandeur and heavenly majesty that has seldom been surpassed. It has been the inspiration for artists down through the ages. These mosaics of Santi Cosma e Damiano are Eastern in character, and represent the final step from Classic to Byzantine art. Italian mosaics before this time are not Byzantine in the true sense, for the Oriental influence does not come to its full blossoming until the sixth century and later in Ravenna.

In the age of Constantine, the essential features of early Christian art are anticipated: its abstraction and flat forms, its frontality, solemnity, and hierarchy, its spiritualism and indifference to individualism and the life of flesh and blood. The idea is always more important than the outward form. We can still feel the meaning of early Christian art, for as communicators of content no artists have ever been more successful.

CHAPTER IV

THE GOLDEN AGE OF BYZANTINE ART

There was no break between early Christian and Byzantine art, for the Byzantine style grew on the same roots and possessed the same characteristics as the style before it, but Byzantine art accentuated the Oriental element so that it became a different and a new style. Byzantine art is Oriental Christian art. It is the art of the great Byzantine Empire that stretched from Turkey and Asia Minor, north into Russia and the Balkans, and west into Italy and France. Byzantine art was stamped by the taste of its patrons, the emperor and high court dignitaries and the abbots of the great monasteries. The imperial court wanted a sumptuous, refined art, and the Church demanded a mystic and dogmatic expression of religion. Byzantine art is flat, two-dimensional, and decorative. It harmonizes with the forms and functions of architecture. The scale and proportions of the decoration are determined by the architectural setting. A horizontal perspective with figures one above the other was used. The size and positions of figures were regulated by their spiritual importance; thus the figure of Christ would be large and in the foreground. All figures were in frontal view. The artist was not aiming at a lifelike image, but sought an interpretation of nature adjusted to a preconceived scale of values understood and accepted by the observer of that era. The flattened figures without weight or substance move in the same rhythm as the columns of the architecture.

If today we do not appreciate the formal stylized manner of Byzantine art, we nevertheless can enjoy the beauty of the color that is one of the most important characteristics of Byzantine art. But here too the artist followed an expressive style and aimed to produce color harmonies rather than color as seen in nature. There were fixed color schemes that belonged to certain persons, and by understanding the key the spectator could know at once who was portrayed. To Christ belonged blue or cherry-red sometimes mixed with gold; blue was the color of the Virgin; St. Peter was represented by yellow and light blue; and St. Paul by blue and claret-red. But everywhere was the rich, sensuous glow and ornamental aspect of the East.

The Byzantine love of flashing color made mosaics a favorite form of decoration. Mosaics consist of small pieces of glass called tesserae. These bits of glass were cemented into the white stucco of the wall with a cementing material, of an inch or more in thickness, formed of lime, broken reed, and crushed white marble. The colors are pure and luminous, with vermilion, reds, emerald greens, blues, and white predominating, but all are set off by accents of gold and silver. The glass of the gold tesserae is yellowish, slightly amethyst, or dark green. The gold was made by laying leaf gold on the glass, on which a thin film of glass was then fused. Tesserae were arranged in rows a short distance apart. Gold tesserae were often set at an angle to the plane of the wall, so that they would flash when light would strike them. To help cement the tesserae, a layer of powdered red tile was sanded on back of the glass. This layer of tile not only aided the cementing but also probably gave the gold more sheen.

The plan of decoration of the Byzantine church was influenced by the imperial palace and the emperor as well as by directions of the Church. Imperial pomp was the inspiration for the big effigies of Christ in the mosaics of the apse, the dome, and the triumphal arch. On the walls of the nave, together with the symbols and decorations, were episodes from the Bible, but now their compositions were also related to the triumphal themes of the emperor, and even included figures of the emperor and the empress. In the sixth century, with the enlargement of the choir, there was more space for decoration, and scenes in which a Eucharistic symbolism was imparted were represented there.

The picture sequences in the baptisteries give the first symbolical interpretations of the functions of places of worship. In the cupola were the sky, sun, moon, and stars surrounded by a glory of angels. On the walls would be a representation of John the Baptist and the Baptism of Christ in the Jordan, with the Holy Spirit on a ray from Heaven with the inscription, "This is my beloved Son, in whom I am well pleased." The miracles of the Old Testament and the Prophets and what they prophesied concerning baptism would complete the picture cycle. This was part of the formal scheme of decoration that was gradually developed and added to through the years. A manual of Byzantine painting, called *The Painter's Guide,* was discovered at Mount Athos, Greece, in the nineteenth century. This was a complete guide for the religious subject matter used by artists in the decoration of churches, and although it does not date before the thirteenth century, a comparison of the directions with the existing paintings and mosaics in Byzantine times shows that a similar guide must have been used much earlier. The manual gives the complete system of iconography for church decoration and the sequence of subjects used to epitomize the divine scheme of salvation, and directs the manner in which historical events, miracles, and parables should be represented, as well as the inscriptions for the scrolls of each Prophet; and how these should be distributed on the walls and cupolas of Byzantine churches. Although the size of some churches limited the subjects used, a similar plan was followed in all church decoration.

In the eighth century the bitter conflict against imagery resulted in the reign of the iconoclasts and the prohibition of human figures in church decoration for two centuries. The popes of Italy did not submit to the edicts of the iconoclasts, and iconoclasm, even in the East, did not lead to a standstill, but merely a new orientation and refreshing change in artistic production based on purely decorative art.

After the end of iconoclasm, the Church officially declared that effigies of Christ and the saints were beneficial to the soul. With this encouragement the use of the Gospel cycles was practiced with more elaboration than before. Such complete illustrations of Gospel cycles are seen in the mosaics of Santa Sophia at Constantinople (Istanbul), in the Church of Nea Moni on the island of Chios, and at Daphni. Although some of the mosaics have been destroyed, the general layout of themes can be discerned. In all these churches there was Christ the Pantocrator in the dome, the Virgin in the apse, with angels, Prophets, and saints on arches, vaults, and niches, and groups of Bible scenes in the nave and narthex.

Although it is thought that the original sixth century mosaic decoration of Santa Sophia consisted of crosses on a ground of gold and four golden cherubim, in the ninth and tenth centuries the church was redecorated according to the traditional Byzantine plan, and the influence of a set iconography of subject matter can be seen in the existing mosaics. Over the door of the narthex is Christ Holy Wisdom seated on a throne and holding the Gospel open to the words "I am the Door: by me, if any man enter in, he shall be saved." Above the door of the south porch are mosaics representing the Virgin and Child to whom Constantine presents a model of the city of Constantinople and Justinian a model of the Church of Santa Sophia. The formal plan is continued in the groups of Apostles, Prophets, and Fathers of the Church. Some of the finest mosaics are seen in these majestic representations of the bishops and Prophets.

But the mosaics are not the only beauty of Santa Sophia. When the church was dedicated, a poem was written for the occasion, and it dwells chiefly on the vastness of the architecture, the beauties of the marble, and the fittings of precious metals. "Everywhere the walls glitter with wondrous designs—the marbles are cut and joined like painted patterns and in stones formed into squares or eight-sided figures—intertwining curves laden with plenteous fruit and baskets and flowers and birds sitting on the twigs, and the curved pattern of a twining vine. Such ornament as this surrounds the church" (as a dado). The capitals of the marble columns have carvings of acanthus and palm, and the floor was also of veined marble. The poet goes on to describe the vaulting formed of many little squares of gold, cemented together. He tells of the silver screen between the nave and the sanctuary, the altar of gold with precious stones, and over the altar the ciborium of silver with silver columns that were carved with leaves. He also describes the altar curtains of gold and silver and bright-colored silk woven with the figure of Christ and the Virgin holding the hands of the emperor. Above the altar hung the crown of the Emperor Constantine, a golden cross and a golden dove, the pyx. When the Crusaders sacked the church during the fourth crusade of 1202–1204, these treasures were destroyed or stolen. Some of them are now at St. Mark's in Venice, as are a pair of bronze doors originally at Santa Sophia.

During the fifth century Ravenna was the capital of the Western Empire, and the Emperor Justinian resided there when in Italy and built lavish palaces and churches decorated with mosaics that remain in good condition today. These mosaics were inspired by the monarchical Christian art of Rome and the reflection of the ceremonial art of the court of Constantinople. The earliest mosaics in Ravenna are in the mausoleum of Galla Placida. Here in the apse is the well-known Good Shepherd with his sheep set within a framework of beautiful blue, green, and gold medallions in the vault. In the dome a large cross is set upon a star-studded background. At the corners are the symbols of the four Evangelists and decorative compositions of deer drinking. The whole interior is a symphony of luminous gold and deep blue; aesthetically it is one of the most stimulating works of art in Christendom. For our enjoyment vistas of infinity are opened up by the white-robed Apostles echoing the pattern of white sheep in the lunette.

The mosaics in the dome of the "Orthodox Church" produce a similar effect. Apostles in white garments studded with gold are set upon a blue ground, and lower down the earthly paradise is depicted in greens and vermilions.

In the Church of St. Apollinare Nuovo, the color scheme is green, white, and purple on gold. The most impressive parts of the mosaic decoration are the rhythmic processions of white-robed martyrs and palm trees alternating with gold and white-robed virgins proceeding with gifts for Christ and for the Virgin. These mosaics are set on the lower walls against a background of gold. Above are the Prophets, Apostles, and Evangelists, and above them, the Gospel scenes in brilliant pure colors.

In the dome of the Church of St. Vitale, Christ sits in glory. Prophets and sacred events relating to the Eucharistic service are pictured in the scenes on the side walls near the altar. But the best-known mosaics in St. Vitale depict the Emperor Justinian and his retinue and the Empress Theodora with her retinue. Each ruler has a nimbus indicating their divine right to rule, and the empress also stands under a canopy, symbol of divinity. The processions carry their gifts of golden Eucharistic vessels, a chalice and a paten, and a jeweled cross. The figures are set against a background of gold and green but seem to be suspended in space and sparkling with light and color. The influence of Constantinople is seen more especially in the mosaics of the Church of St. Apollinare in Classe where a large jeweled "Cross of Jerusalem" with a bust of Christ is set on a field of stars in the dome. On either side are sheep that represent the Apostles, and below is a beautiful garden scene and another decorative border of sheep. On the triumphal arch is a bust of Christ and the four Evangelists.

All these mosaics reflect a formalism of courtly and ecclesiastical ritual. Christ is represented as a king, Mary as a queen; they wear royal robes and sit, forbidding and expressionless, on their thrones. The Apostles and saints move in slow, stately rhythms like the processions of court ceremonies and ecclesiastical order. Everything is transformed into an awe-inspiring regal pageant, beautiful beyond compare. But the beauty is that of another world created by decorative pattern and color. The figures are flat; they are not people but abstract beauty of rhythms and color harmony and composition. They are there to enhance the beauty and proportion of the architecture, and no matter how great they are in their own artistic right they take their place as an integral part of the whole structure. Their lack of material reality fits them to the transcendental content of Christianity.

The churches described above were built in the two centuries before iconoclasm. Great church decoration was also carried on in Constantinople, Ravenna, Rome, on the islands of Greece, and in Sicily during the centuries after iconoclasm. The mosaics in the Church of Nea Moni on the island of Chios and at Daphni date from the twelfth century. At Daphni, a great imperialist Christ Pantocrator is centered in the gold dome. The mosaics in Sicily at the cathedral of Cefalu, Monreale, and at Palermo also date from the eleventh and twelfth centuries. In the apse at Monreale, against a gold ground, a majestic Christ Judge of the World is robed in blue. Below are the Virgin, angels, and Apostles. The significance of the scenes is told in the esoteric Byzantine manner, with inner meanings given to costumes, attributes, and gestures.

The best examples of twelfth and thirteenth century mosaics are in Torcello, Murano, and St. Mark's, Venice. The mosaics at Torcello are typically Byzantine. In the dome of the apse a huge figure of the Virgin floats dramatically against the shimmering gold background and above the row of Apostles. Facing this decoration are scenes of the Crucifixion, Resurrection, and Last Judgment. This is one of the earliest and most interesting representations of the Last Judgment. Although many of the mosaics of St. Mark's are late in date and not so fine aesthetically as those mentioned above, the church itself, which was fashioned on the architectural plan of the Church of the Holy Apostles at Constantinople, is composed of domes that form a cross, and is one of the most colorful of late Byzantine monuments. The mosaics of St. Mark's are not Byzantine in conception. There are no imperial processions or portraits of emperors; instead the inspiration for the scenes came from manuscript Bible illustrations. There are typical decorative landscapes with hills, trees, and buildings, and the scenes are enlivened with local color and realism, including groups of quail, a water jug, camels, and pyramids. Reality is created by a poetic, almost sentimental approach, and colors are softer and lighter and more varied in tone, but still within the bounds of art related to architecture. These late Italian mosaics show more realism, individual inventiveness, and imagination, and point to the next period in the development of Church art.

Fresco painting was also employed for the decoration of Byzantine churches. While many of the churches in Constantinople and Rome must have been painted at the same time that others were decorated with costlier mosaics, it is in the poorer churches of the provinces, in monasteries, and in outlying parts of the empire, such as Greece, Cypress, the Balkans, Russia, and Cappadocia, that the bulk of Byzantine fresco art is to be found today. Long practice made the Byzantine artist an expert in church painting, since from the time of the passing of iconoclasm every church had all its available surfaces covered. However, only fragments remain of the painting done before the eleventh century. The frescoes in the churches of Yugoslavia, Serbia, and southern Greece of the eleventh century to the fourteenth century are especially interesting and well preserved. They follow the strict Byzantine layout and flat, formal style of painting, but some of the pictures contain detail and meticulous brushwork that relates them more to the small portable painting or religious icon than to church decoration. Figures show modeling, and the faces have human expressions of sorrow and pain, sympathy and compassion. But the work lacks the brilliance and fervor of the early period. And although these scenes are more understandable to many persons today, they do not have the monumental quality of early mosaics.

Byzantine sculpture and minor arts were governed by the same rules and show the same characteristics as the mosaics and frescoes, and all are bound together in a oneness by their reliance upon a formal symmetry in design, ceremonialism of arrangement, and the use of dogmatic symbolism in their treatment of subject matter. Although sculpture was not so important in the Byzantine Age as it was in periods following, there were sarcophagi made in Asia Minor during the era, and the capitals of columns, cornices, pulpits, and other architectural stonework are carved. The sarcophagi continue the figure work and Bible stories, but much of the other sculpture was purely conventional or geometrical, made up of such delightful Oriental motifs as birds, animals, leaves, and vines or abstract symbols and monograms. The many-colored marble columns of Santa Sophia, with their sculptured capital designs of lily, acanthus, and palm leaves, are some of the most characteristic examples of Byzantine art.

The beautiful carved alabaster fifth century ciborium columns of St. Mark's, Venice, represent one of the important monuments of early Christian art. According to C. R. Morey, they depict the earliest existing cycle of the life of Christ in Christian sculpture. The episodes are arranged against a background of columns and arches, and each is identified with a Latin inscription. Especially interesting is the scene of the Crucifixion with a lamb upon the Cross, which is an early Crucifixion type. The columns were brought from Constantinople to St. Mark's after the sack of Constantinople.

The same cyclic representations of Bible subjects are also seen in the beautiful ivory carvings on triptychs, boxes, pyxes, book covers, and plaques. Such familiar symbols as the Good Shepherd, the fish, the anchor, the Chi Rho, and the well-known symbols of the Evangelists are seen, as well as complete events from the Old Testament, including Abraham and the Three Angels, and also the life of Christ. There were seldom any portrayals of saints, popes, or other ecclesiastical characters. However, there are some interesting ivory carvings that illustrate the ritual and episcopal ceremonials such as the ordination of a deacon, the blessing of oils, the bishop anointing a child, the blessing of the font, and the consecration of a church. In the Louvre is a plaque that shows an archbishop at Mass, and in the British Museum is a plaque of an archbishop vested in chasuble. Ivory plaques and diptychs were used in the service of the Church not only as bindings for the Gospel and other sacred books but also for covering the sides of caskets, pyxes, and holy-water buckets. Diptychs that contained memoranda of the living and the dead were placed on the altar and read from in the Mass. The other side of the diptych was carved with a Biblical scene.

Some of the earliest Christian ivory carvings are the cylindrical pyxes that date from the fourth and fifth centuries. One such pyx shows the young beardless Christ seated on a throne with His hand raised in benediction, and near Him St. Peter and St. Paul and the other Apostles. In another group appears the Sacrifice of Abraham and the hand of God issuing from the clouds. The expressions, attitudes, and grouping of the figures are similar to those on the sarcophagi of the same century.

There were centers of ivory carving in Alexandria, Rome, Antioch, Milan, Constantinople, and France. The style of workmanship varied with the location, but the same subject matter, consisting of the well-known Bible themes, is to be found throughout the years and in all geographical centers. The ivories of the fifth and sixth centuries of Constantinople have a conservatism of design and fine workmanship of a cold finished type that relates them to the Classic style of early Christian art.

Certain pieces of early ivory with religious subject matter are particularly important. The most famous series of ivory carvings are on the plaques of the great chair known as the Cathedra of Maximus in the Archiepiscopal Palace in Ravenna. On the front panels of this chair are figures of John the Baptist and the four Evangelists. On the sides of the seat is the history of Joseph, and the panels on the chair's back depict the life of Christ. Christ throughout the series of carvings is represented beardless, with short hair, which is according to the Classic Greek tradition. However, an Eastern origin is suggested for the Cathedra by the borders of grapes and leaves mingled with birds and animals that connect the panels.

An ivory casket at Brescia dates from the fourth century. On the very small spaces of this box is a cycle of thirty-six scenes from the Bible, beginning with Moses receiving the Law and ending with the story of the life of Christ.

A Rhenish-Byzantine shrine of the twelfth century is in the form of a Byzantine church in the shape of a Greek cross surmounted by a dome. It is richly enameled and gilded and has inset plaques of ivory with scenes of the visit of the Magi, the Virgin and Child, the Crucifixion and the Resurrection; and ivory figures of Christ and the Apostles and Prophets are set in the arches.

The minor arts of the Byzantine period also included beautiful silverwork. The craft of the goldsmith was one of the oldest of all time, dating from the early dynasties of Egypt, Assyria, and Babylonia, and finally culminating in the silver, gold, and enamel work of the Byzantines of the early centuries after Christ's birth. The earliest liturgical objects of Christian usage that exist today include the famous Chalice of Antioch, dating from the early centuries of the Christian Era, and a silver cross and silver book covers with figures of saints holding books or crosses and with borders of grapevine, birds, and peacocks. These date from the fifth or sixth century and were found with the Chalice of Antioch. Other early liturgical objects include the silver chalices ornamented in *repoussé* designs of saints and large crosses framed in arcades, silver plates, and finely proportioned silver candlesticks. Byzantine liturgical silver also included small altar crosses, silver patens, hanging lamps, and Eucharistic spoons. A group of fine Byzantine silver dishes from Cyprus that date from the seventh century show scenes from the life of David.

During the Middle Ages the most talented artists produced works of art and vessels for use in the Church service. Although existing inventories of monasteries and cathedrals and the records of early writers tell us of the vast treasure of chalices, ciboriums, reliquaries, candlesticks, and crosses, a great deal of Church treasure perished, and comparatively few pieces have been preserved. The treasury of St. Mark's, Venice, has some of the finest examples of tenth century Byzantine goldsmiths' work. The famous Pala d'Oro, or altarpiece of gold and enamel, the enamel gold and jeweled icon of the Archangel Michael, and the rock crystal chalice are notable examples. There were also many Byzantine gold crosses with enamel plaques.

Liturgical objects of the Byzantine and Romanesque periods relied on color and richness of materials for their beauty. Articles were accented with enamel plaques and studded with precious colored gems. The chalice is low and heavy in comparison with chalices of later date. The famous French Romanesque golden chalice made for the Abbot Suger of Saint-Denis dates from about 1140. It is made of sardonyx with bands of gold filigree, medallions of embossed gold, and is studded with gems and pearls. The chalice is heavy-jointed, with a massive knob, and the cup is wide and outcurving.

Another important liturgical object was the Eucharistic dove made of copper gilt and enamel. This was a pyx to hold the wafer or Host and was set on a circular frame and hung over the altar on a pulley. The ciborium was a goblet-shaped vessel surmounted by a cross. It was used for keeping and distributing the Host.

The grandeur and elegance of the Byzantine period is nowhere better illustrated than in the colorful enamels. These enamels were made by the cloisonné method. Strips of gold were soldered to a plate of hammered gold to outline the design. Then heated pulverized glass was poured in the spaces. The method and the limitations of the technique fitted the Byzantine conventions of dignity and restraint in design and boldness of pure color. Such colors as blues, purples, reds, greens, yellows, white, and flesh pink were made by mixing oxides with the ground glass. The subjects included heads of Christ and the Apostles in circles or rectangular plaques made to decorate crosses, book covers, reliquaries, or chalices. The Byzantine enamels in existence include those from the eighth to the thirteenth centuries. Those in the Morgan Collection at the Metropolitan Museum date from the tenth century to the thirteenth century and include a beautiful reliquary box with scenes of the Crucifixion with the Virgin and St. John and the moon and sun above, and in the border are fourteen busts of saints. In the Vatican collection is a reliquary cross with scenes of the Birth of Christ. In addition to the figure plaques there are also plaques with animals and beautiful border decorations of geometric patterns. These small enamels set on a gold ground are very closely related to the mosaics set against the gold backgrounds on the walls and domes of the Byzantine churches and serve to illustrate the uniformity of all Byzantine art.

Christian art was brought to England in the sixth century by Columba to the Isle of Iona and by St. Augustine to southern England. The sculpture, metalwork, and manuscript illumination dating from the seventh century give evidence of outstanding workmanship. The great stone crosses of Bewcastle and Ruthwell are examples of the interesting work by native sculptors that also shows the influence of Byzantine style and iconography as well as the typical interlaced ornament of the North. But the most characteristic British Christian art expression at this time was the manuscript illuminations made in Northumbria, Ireland, and later in southern England at Canterbury and Winchester. The Lindisfarne Gospels and the Book of Durrow with crude figures and decorative ornament composed of heavy interlacings and angular patterns date from the seventh century, and the Book of Kells dates from the ninth century. Illuminated manuscripts were also painted in similar style in southern England, in Scandinavia, and on the Continent.

To understand and appreciate Byzantine art we must attempt

to see it in the conditions that it reflects and in the limitations of the age. The fusion of Greek, Roman, and Oriental elements gives it imagination and spontaneity, but these qualities were smothered by the conventions of the Church. Nature was lost sight of, and in its place we are taken out of this world into a tranquil, mystic, and emotional realm of the imagination that reflects the spirit of the religion of the age. The gold backgrounds and jeweled crosses of Byzantine art are used to overwhelm the soul with the splendor of mystical light. Byzantine Christian art exerted its influence upon Renaissance times.

CHAPTER V

THE GLORY OF ROMANESQUE

God dwelleth in a light that none may come nigh.

—St. Paul, I Timothy 6:16

While the Byzantine Empire was rising to great heights in the East, strife and decay increased at Rome. There were barbarian invasions from the North, and these successive barbarian onslaughts finally brought about the fall of Rome. The Latin Empire was not restored to power again until A.D. 800, when Charlemagne was crowned Holy Roman Emperor and established order for a short time. Charlemagne sought to revive the ideals of Classic and Byzantine antiquity. At Aix-la-Chapelle a cathedral modeled after St. Vitale at Ravenna was built, and an academy and artists' workshop to recreate Classic and Byzantine art were founded. The ivory carvings and other minor arts of the Carolingian period imitated the Byzantine, and churches were restored after antique models, with painted frescoes of Bible cycles.

The architecture of the Carolingian royal abbey churches was planned to reassert the divine right of kings. Thus the towered façade or king's gate was erected at the entrance of the royal abbey churches where the king resided, and the features of Roman and Constantinople architecture, such as the city gate, towered façade, cupola, baldachin, and ciborium, which gave significant meaning to the political aims of the king over the Pope and the Church, were incorporated into the architecture. The arcade, king's gallery with statues, and round "sun window" were all used to emphasize the divine importance of the king who sat in the western apse while Christ was enthroned in fresco or mosaic in the eastern apse. The towers at the four corners of the church were symbols of the royal camp of the emperor. This imperial concept of ritual and architecture was transformed into a Christian rite.

The architecture, painting, and sculpture of the period are a continuance of Christian antique and Byzantine, but Celtic and

German influences are to be seen in the motifs of the decorative patterns of manuscript illumination. The products of the Carolingian workshops, whether manuscript paintings, metalwork, or ivory carvings, were all comparatively small in scale so that they could be packed and moved by the constantly shifting royal court. The Carolingian period produced a considerable treasury of these small objects of art, and many exist today, especially manuscripts and ivory carvings. The famous Utrecht Psalter, the Ebbo Gospel Book, the Breton Gospel Book, and the Vivian Bible are all manuscripts that belong to this period.

After the death of Charlemagne, Western Europe and the Church sank to their lowest level, and Christian art, except for the Ottoman period in Germany, slumbered until awakened in the tenth century by the efforts of the Benedictine monastic system. In the East the Classic and Oriental influences had combined to form the Byzantine; in the West the two older influences were now combined with the barbaric Teutonic native influence to form the Romanesque. There was also a difference in the point of view. Byzantine art was mystic, contemplative, and sophisticated; Romanesque was an emotional, ecstatic religious expression and had more originality and vitality.

The new religious enthusiasm culminated in the Crusades and pilgrimages that in turn influenced the spread and development of Christian art. Crusades were made to the Holy Sepulcher in Jerusalem. Pilgrimages were also made to Rome and to Spain, and often the pilgrim made the tour of all three holy places. The widespread treasuring of sacred relics also led to a continual movement of devout pilgrims back and forth across the Continent. In the eleventh century the journey to the shrine of Santiago de Compostella in Spain ranked in fame with pilgrimages to Rome and Jerusalem. Not only did the Benedictines of Cluny supervise the building of monasteries along the route, but through their preaching they held men's minds in a state of constant religious excitement. Preaching the end of the world and the Last Judgment, they produced an apocalyptic mood of escapism and a yearning for death that were given visible form in the subject matter of the sculptured church portals. Handicraft workshops were set up at Cluny and at Monte Cassino, at Fulda, St. Gall, and Hildesheim in Germany, and at Winchester and Canterbury, England. Indeed, too much stress cannot be put on the influence of the Benedictines and the importance of the pilgrimages in the development of Romanesque art. Especially in France the monasteries supplanted the court as the cultural and intellectual center of the empire.

The strange beauty of Italian Romanesque art that developed in Lombardy was influenced by the Teutonic from the North, and in southern Italy the Romanesque was influenced by the Byzantine and Islamic cultures as well as by the inheritance of antiquity. The Teutonic influence extended to Rome, Ravenna, and Venice. Architecture in Lombardy acquired characteristics from both Germany and France. It took from the North such architectural forms as the detached nave and the low triforium, as well as the groined vault, and at the same time created its own forms of the baptistery and separate campanile that were generally adopted throughout Italy. The bells in the campanile had liturgical significance. They rang for the offices twelve times a day—the number of the bells indicating the service. Teutonic influence is seen in Italian Romanesque churches in the grotesque shapes of animals carved on the capitals of columns, pulpits, tympanums, and reliefs of church porches. Italian Romanesque churches were built in all the little villages of Lombardy, especially in the Lake Como district, but the best-known monuments of Italian Romanesque are the Basilica of San Ambrogio in Milan, the cathedrals of Pisa and Lucca, and the cathedrals in Cefalu, Monreale, and Palermo, Sicily. The most important Romanesque church in Italy, San Ambrogio in Milan, is a plain building flanked on either side by a square tower. In the interior it is a Christian basilica without a transverse aisle, but it is roofed over with ribbed vaulting supported by clustered piers, and is one of the earliest examples of these innovations. Other Romanesque churches, such as the Parma Baptistery, are notable for decorated and arcaded façades and geometric and grotesque animal designs of dark and light marble, both on their interior and exterior walls.

These Italian Romanesque churches with rhythmically colonnaded façades, often including early rose windows with pierced designs of animals, and arched doorways with primitive carvings of men and animals interlaced with vines, leaves, and strapwork arabesques, give an almost forbidding atmosphere of barbaric ferocity. There are few Biblical scenes on the exterior stonework except for an occasional Tree of Life, but there are Biblical episodes on the relief decoration of the bronze doors of the cathedrals at Pisa, Monreale, Trani, and San Zeno at Verona. Carving in the interiors of churches was concentrated on the capitals of columns, wall plaques, and the impressive stone pulpits. Stone inlay or Cosmati work was applied to porches, floors, parapets, canopies, pulpits, thrones, and Easter candelabra. Stone inlay is combined with marble sculpture in the pulpits at the cathedrals of Ravello, Salerno, and Sessa Aurunca. Beautiful carving is displayed on tall Easter candelabra, such as the candelabra in the cathedral at Gaeta with its shaft carved with panels of episodes from the life of Christ. Fresco wall decorations, altar pieces, triptychs, and huge painted wooden crucifixes were also produced in large numbers in the Romanesque mid-twelfth century in Rome and Tuscany.

Romanesque architecture in Germany included notable churches in the Rhine Valley at Cologne, Speyer, and at Hildesheim. St. Michael's at Hildesheim was begun early in 1100. It consists of two apses, two transepts, and two chancels. The nave is divided into three squares with the aisles separated from the nave by arcades supported by pillars and columns. On the exterior are two towers with spires, and over both transverse crossings are turrets. The church was built by St. Bernward, the bishop who was also responsible for the beautiful bronze doors that depict episodes from the Bible. The two-tower façade originated in Germany and was also used by the Normans, and from there the idea was carried to England and appears in the English Norman cathedrals and abbey churches of Winchester, Ely, and Durham.

Romanesque began in England with the construction of Durham Cathedral. Because of rib vaults the nave of the cathedral appears higher than it is. The pillars of the arcades are simple and overpoweringly bulky, and their ornament consists of abstract zigzags, flutes, and lozenges, which are typical English Romanesque motifs. With its mighty central tower and two entrance towers, Durham Cathedral is one of the most impressive sights in England.

English Romanesque sculpture grew out of the tradition of English sculpture, which runs an unbroken sequence from the great seventh century crosses of Ruthwell and Bewcastle. The subject matter of English Romanesque sculpture followed the crude designs of Norman and Carolingian influences rather than the Biblical cycles. Decoration on English Romanesque tympanums consists of grotesque animals, crosses, and simple designs of the Tree of Life, Agnus Dei, and crude Crucifixions. The arches were bordered with cables, zigzags, dentils, lozenges, and stars, and the capitals of columns were of block or scalloped design or carved with animals, lions, winged dragons, fish, and other grotesque beasts. On the tympanums of some of the larger cathedrals, such as Ely and Rochester, and monasteries like Malmsbury scenes are depicted such as Christ in glory surrounded by a mandorla. In Chichester Cathedral are reliefs depicting stories from the life of Christ. Fine carvings are also to be seen at Westminster, Rochester, and Lincoln cathedrals. These carvings follow the iconography of the Continental mainstream and were adapted from manuscript illustrations, but the work is essentially English and differs from the Continental in style and technique. A distinctive product of English Romanesque art was the carved stone and black Tournai marble fonts. There were also retables, pectoral crosses, crucifixes, book covers, altars, and candlesticks of metal. The Gloucester candlestick in the Victoria and Albert Museum, South Kensington, London, with an arabesque pattern of animals and human forms, is an outstanding example of English Romanesque metalwork.

In the tenth century there were schools of manuscript illumination at Winchester, Bury St. Edmonds, and Canterbury. Full-page scenes of the Bible stories have borders of acanthus leaves, rosettes, and trelliswork. One of the finest manuscripts of this date was the copy of the Utrecht Psalter made at Canterbury about the year 1000. Although many fine illuminated manuscripts have been preserved, few wall paintings have survived. These are mostly in the south of England at St. Botolph's Church in Hardham, in Coombes, Sussex, and in the chapels of Canterbury Cathedral.

If the Romanesque style was widespread and varied in different countries, the same is true of France, where the expression of the style varied from one province to another. Yet taken together it is enough of a unit on which to base our general study of the Romanesque, for there is a homogeneity in the architecture, decoration, and iconography of the period. In the Romanesque architecture of Lombardy and the Normans, the innovations and changes were mainly structural. French Romanesque adopted the use of rib vaulting and the decorated entrance façade with its two towers. Roman order was everywhere apparent, and the Lombard arcade and the simple forms of square, circle, or semicircle determined the dimensions of the walls, arches, and vaults. But French Romanesque, through the influence of the monastery at Cluny, also brought about changes in the church interiors that were required by the liturgical needs and traditions of the order. Generally speaking, the interior plan followed that which had been gradually evolved during the Carolingian Age: a nave with two aisles, a cross transept with a dome and classical cupola at the crossing, and a simple form of ambulatory with radiating chapels. But these features were altered and enlarged to meet functional and liturgical requirements, such as the growing worship of saints and the custom of every priest saying Mass every day so that more altars and more chapels were needed. The focus of monastery life was the altar and the choir, and this was the center around which the church was built and all decoration concentrated. The altar was placed in an aureole of columns at the end of the long nave. The altar itself was usually a slab of stone with columns and solid stonework between. The color of the church was also concentrated about the altar. There were frescoes in the apse, embroidered curtains, painted sculptures, and gold and silver or bronze altar frontals. Silver ciboriums were often built over the altar, and jeweled chalices and reliquaries, Gospel books, and candlesticks were used on the altar; and hanging above the altar a dove-shaped pyx of gold, enamels, and jewels held the reserved wafers. This place was set apart for the rich setting of the Mass. The choir of brethren so necessary for the chanting sat in stalls near the altar. There were usually twelve or more brethren, but at Cluny there were as many as 450. To accommodate the large number, the choir and transept were enlarged. Pilgrimage churches also needed large spaces to accommodate the great number of pilgrims. Thus aisles were sometimes increased to as many as five and were lengthened and prolonged around the apse and formed an ambulatory with radiating chapels that took care of extra services and provided a pathway for processions of the relics of the saint. This system of ambulatory and radiating chapels unified the plan of the eastern end of the church. Again, the aisles might be run past the transept and end in an apse in which an altar would be placed. Where towers were planned they were designed to end in spires; thus the exterior as well as the interior of the Romanesque church varied widely from the early Christian church because of structural and liturgical needs. The Romanesque church was erected not only to serve the faithful but also as a monument to the greater glory of God, and it was a symbol of supreme power and authority. The eleventh century was a world based on unconditional devotion to God without skepticism. The relics were venerated, and their authenticity or healing power was not questioned. Medieval religion had strength, fantastic ecstasy, aesthetic beauty, dignity, and splendor, and Romanesque church architecture with its massive construction and dim lighting had an air of mystery that contributed to the intuitive and emotional understanding of a religion that was viewed as a mystery.

There are various forms of Romanesque church art that demand our attention. There are the sculpture at the portals and on the walls of the façade and the carved ornamentation on the pillars and supports of the beautiful capitals. Then there are painted frescoes on walls and vaults and the plastic and painted ornamentation of altars, fonts, and images, as well as the gold and silver articles of liturgical usage. There arc also bronze doors and stained glass, and illuminated manuscripts that add to the wealth of the beauty of medieval holiness.

Sculpture more than anything else breathes the spirit of Romanesque art. The beautiful portals with their sculptured semicircular tympanums proclaim the transcendency of Romanesque vision. Within this semicircle is placed a triangular composition with the highest figure in the center. The subject matter, which was of three types, depicted an invisible world and was designed to prepare man for entrance into the sanctuary. The first type represented is that of Christ in Glory or the Christ of the Apocalypse as shown in the tympanum over the door of the Abbey of Moissac and in the royal west portal of Chartres Cathedral.

The second type of tympanum depicts the Last Judgment, where Christ sits as judge between the blessed and the damned. At Beaulieu the figure of Christ is seated with outstretched arms that repeat the lines of the off-center cross in the background. Below are two wide borders of monsters. At the Conques portal, Christ sits within a mandorla, with stars denoting the heavens, and is surrounded by twenty-four figures of the elders with explanatory texts, while at Autun a gigantic majestic figure of Christ stands within a mandorla with the sun on the right and the moon on the left. Another type of tympanum depicts the Ascension. This type is found at Toulouse and at Chartres. A similar composition in the tympanum between the narthex and the nave at Vézelay represents the scene of Pentecost. A fourth type of portal dedicated to the Virgin appeared at the end of the twelfth century and is carved on the tympanum of Senlis and on that in Bourges.

One of the most distinctive features of the Romanesque church is its columns, and there are literally hundreds of them, starting with the exterior columns at the doorways. In the interior were columns at the altar and ambulatory columns around the choir, as well as the rows of smaller columns above the choir and apse and at the window frames. Columns also marked the archways of the cloister. All these columns were based on Corinthian forms, but the capitals were intricately carved with animal and leaf motifs, and figure sculpture in episodes from the Bible. At Autun the Apocryphal legends and the Gospel stories are illustrated. Figures are often crowded together, as on the early sarcophagi, and details such as St. Peter's key are larger than the saint himself, but all fits into the shape and form of the column and takes its place in the general architectural scheme. The metamorphosis of human figures into columns that reached its culmination in the columns of Prophets, kings, and queens of the Old Law in the portals of Chartres are also to be seen at Le Mans and in the central pillar at the portal of Beaulieu where the elongated figure of the Prophet seems more a part of the column than a figure.

Never was the sculptor so important or so necessary as in Romanesque art. In addition to sculpture in stone there were carved wooden figures and metalwork figures of saints. Each church had an image of its patron saint worked in gold, silver, or copper over a wooden structure. These images, hieratic and formal in character, served as reliquaries and were set upon the altar and carried around the church at great feasts. These images of saints were called "majesties," and the famous golden majesty of St. Foy is still to be seen in the church at Conques. There were also crosses and crucifixes, croziers, candlesticks, chalices, and Gospel book covers decorated with enamel and jewels by the goldsmith or silversmith. The famous Cross of Mathilda, the Cross of Lothair, and the Cross and Crozier of Bernward of Hildesheim are of the Romanesque period. The monk Theophilus in his treatise *Upon Divers Arts* instructs the artist to "set thyself with all the might of thy soul to complete that which is yet lacking in the gear of the Lord's house without which the divine mysteries and the ministeries of God's service may not stand; such as chalices, candlesticks, thuribles, chrism vases, crewets, shrines for holy relics, crosses, missals, and such like, which the necessary use of the ecclesiastical order requireth."

The walls of Romanesque churches were decorated with painted frescoes. Fresco painting was of two kinds: *buon fresco,* which was done with pure pigment mixed with water and painted on the wet lime surface of the wall, and *fresco secco,* in which pigments were mixed with lime and milk and applied to a dry plaster wall. The colors were limited by the process and the pigments. Color of backgrounds was usually blue, red, or yellow with bands and stripes used decoratively. The illustrations of the Gospel, Psalter, and Sacramentary were sources for many fresco designs. Manuscripts of the fifth and sixth centuries were also used, as well as the famous Apocalypse de Saint-Sever, which was one of a group of illustrated Romanesque Apocalypse manuscripts which include a group of Beatus apocalypses made by the Christian artists of Spain. In these Spanish apocalyptic writings there is a primitive handling of color and subject matter that gives them an exotic strangeness. Other famous apocalyptic writings were the Bamberg and Trier apocalypses made in Germany. Apocalyptic themes were also painted by Anglo-Norman artists in England. These form only one group of the many beautiful illustrated manuscripts of Romanesque times. In the actual painting and use of colors a guide similar to the Byzantine manual of painting had considerable influence on fresco painting. There is evidence that this instruction from the manual was often followed: "When you desire to paint the walls of a church first draw near the summit of the cupola a circle of different colours like a rainbow seen on clouds in rainy weather [the aureole or mandorla]. In the center represent Christ blessing. He bears the Gospel on his breast. Paint this inscription: 'Jesus Christ, the Almighty.'" Romanesque frescoes repeated the general subject matter and arrangement of Byzantine mosaics and paintings. The complete formal hierarchical scheme of subject matter was never fully adopted in the Romanesque, but focal points in the church were still reserved for Church dogma. In the dome of the apse a huge figure of Christ—Majestas Domini—replaced the Pantocrator or Judge of the Byzantines. Christ is seated in a mandorla with book, and His hand is raised in blessing. The Last Judgment was usually painted on the west wall of the church, and the lower parts of the wall were painted in imitation of curtains and hangings.

Saint-Savin-sur-Gartempe, a Benedictine abbey founded by Charlemagne, is the largest surviving Romanesque church of the early period in France. It is notable both for its lofty architecture and for the unique wall and ceiling frescoes. The vaults of the roof are covered with scenes from the Old Testament. Romanesque iconography included the cycle of the Twelve Feasts of the Church, namely: the Annunciation, Nativity, Presentation, Baptism, Transfiguration, Raising of Lazarus, Entry into Jerusalem, Crucifixion, Harrowing of Hell or Anastasis, Ascension, Pentecost, and Dormition of the Virgin. Apocalyptic visions were also favorite subjects. These included the Enthroned Lamb on the Book of Seven Seals, the Seven Candlesticks, the symbols of the Evangelists, the Four Rivers of Paradise, and the Twenty-four Elders offering their crowns to God. Actual quotations from the decrees of theological thought and interpretations of Church scholars were painted into the scenes along with realistic episodes of daily life, animal symbols, and the Labors of the Months. Frescoes are also found in Romanesque churches in Germany, Sicily, England, Scandinavia, and Spain. The Spanish frescoes from Catalonia have been gathered into the art museums of Barcelona, Vich, and Solsona, and are more numerous than those from any other part of the Continent. Spanish Romanesque frescoes show both Moorish and Arab influences, as well as influences from France and Italy. The themes of these paintings include the Last Judgment, cycles of the Childhood and Passion of Christ, a limited number of lives of patron saints, and such courtly scenes as Nebuchadnezzar and his montebanks and David with his musicians. The style is linear, with heavy contour lines, and the color is dark—terra cotta, dull deep blue, and ochers predominating. In Spanish Romanesque churches there were also painted wooden altar frontals and panels, and similar frontals were painted in the Romanesque-Gothic Stave churches of Norway.

Because of the Church, which had become the only source for commissions of art, the Romanesque style is an art solely concerned with the expression of the spiritual inner vision. It was completely dominated by its subject matter, and that subject matter was God. Romanesque art was not an aesthetic enjoyment, but an extension of worship—a votive offering—a sacrificial gift. The symbolism of the Romanesque was not generally understood by the people, but it put them in a solemn and religious frame of mind. Romanesque art is emotional and expressive because of its mystic and religious characteristics. It is a vigorous art, but since it is based on simple forms it is an art of calmness and gravity. Although the human figure is used and the subject matter is narrative, all is related to the architecture by means of abstraction and a rigid formalism. Animals, foliage, and the human figure fit into spaces and accord with the total pattern of architecture rather than with reality. Everything is stereotyped; the mountains are stiff, trees are small, and hands are long, gesticulating, and expressive, and all reveals a sacred scene within a sacred world.

The source and inspiration of Romanesque art were in the past, and we see the influence of both Greek and Byzantine art, and of Oriental fabrics in the symmetry of animals facing each other as in Persian silks and the stone carvings of Chaldea and Assyria. The eagle as a religious symbol came from the East. The hieratic quality of the figures of the Virgin and of Christ comes from Byzantine art, while the Syrian Oriental interpretation of Christ with a long beard is the Christ of Romanesque art. But a more direct influence came from manuscripts, especially the Apocalypse de Saint-Sever written in A.D. 784. In the illustrations of this manuscript we see the interpretation of the Apocalypse as carved on the portal of the Abbey of Moissac. From manuscript painting comes the use of the mandorla or aureole about the figure of Christ, the winged demons of the Inferno, and the Ascension scene at Toulouse. In all the garments of the figures there is a calligraphy of folds that gives a beautiful rhythm and grace. Romanesque art was also influenced by the bestiaries and herbals. Another element in Romanesque art was the use of simple barbaric motifs—of squares, circles, triangles, and interwoven geometric patterns that gave vigor and contrast. These barbaric motifs are seen especially in German, Norman, and English Romanesque sculptures.

Although Romanesque drew from the past, it also gave much to the future. In the Romanesque period many of the features that are distinctly Gothic were developed, and the Gothic, although it did not originate them, combined them for a new aesthetic purpose. Romanesque art is not only a transition into Gothic but is of itself a vital expressive art that is only now receiving its due share of recognition; yet the men who created this art did not consider themselves artists. They were religious believers who invented images and symbols to present truths that lay beyond human experience.

CHAPTER VI

GOTHIC CHURCH ART

"All great art is prayer."
—John Ruskin

The Gothic spirit that permeated the works of art of almost all Western Europe from the middle of the twelfth century to the end of the fourteenth was brought about by an intellectual reawakening. The Carolingian Renaissance had been in the court and palace school; that of the tenth and eleventh centuries centered in the monasteries; but the flowering of the twelfth century that produced Gothic art was centered in the cathedrals in the midst of towns and cities. The influence of the great bishops of Canterbury, Winchester, Chartres, Le Mans, Laon, and Toledo brought about a revival of Latin and the philosophy, mathematics, and astronomy of the Greeks and Arabs that was expressed in the term "scholasticism." Another decisive change was the rise of the artisans and merchants, and their formation into guilds and professional groups. Gothic art is urban and bourgeois in contrast to the monastic aristocratic Romanesque. Cathedrals were built with the wealth of towns, not individuals, and religion was humanized and emotionalized for the masses.

The mood of Gothic art was a type of emotional mysticism brought about by a kinship of the human and the spiritual. The cathedrals with their soaring spires reproduced the spiritual vision of the age. The figures of Christ, the Virgin, and the angels were a combination of transcendental mystery and human sensitiveness. Christ has human tenderness; the Virgin and angels are youthful, radiant, and smiling with beatific countenances. The faces of the statues are serene; they appear neither to suffer anxiety nor to worry about the infinite.

There were two outstanding personalities that helped fashion the Gothic Age. The Abbot Suger of Saint-Denis had influence because he was close to the King of France and controlled the expenditure of great sums. Suger sought to make the Church of Saint-Denis one of splendor by the use of sumptuous materials—gold, precious stones, ivories, mosaics, and stained glass—as well as by the perfection of craftsmanship. The choir and ambulatory of Saint-Denis, the portals and the design of the Tree of Jesse window—all initiated by Suger—are features that were influential in creating the Gothic cathedral. The other leader who helped determine the character of Gothic design was St. Bernard, the head of the Order of Cistercians. The Cistercian Order had been founded in protest against the worldly sumptuousness of the Church. The rules of the order forbade the use of sculpture, façade towers, columns, and stained-glass windows. Cistercian churches were simple and austere; built in the form of the cross, they relied on beauty of proportions for effect.

In Gothic art the conception of God wholly independent of the world gives way to that of a God who is present and working in all nature. This new feeling for nature was the theme of the Franciscans, who counted every creature as "brother," and it was also expressed in the writings of St. Thomas who said, "God enjoys all things, for each accords with His essence." Gothic naturalism in art manifests itself in the use of forms of nature in the foliated capitals of cathedral columns. Leaves and flowers are chosen for their natural beauty. They are simplified, but their structure and appearance are that of natural growing forms. It was a love of nature rather than symbolic meaning that prompted their use. The human form was also portrayed with characteristic lifelike movements. Romanesque figures were abstract; Gothic figures have individuality and characteristic details. But while the Gothic artist looked to nature and life itself for inspiration, he still relied on symbolism for the interpretation of subject matter and he also reflected the elegant refinement of the age.

A tour of Gothic church art is no small undertaking, since it means dealing with almost every medium of art expression from architecture and massive sculpture down to articles of liturgical usage, such as a chalice or altar cross, and articles for private devotions, such as Books of Hours and small ivory triptychs. It also means visiting almost every country of Europe; for the course of Gothic art was not confined to France and England, but extended to Italy, Germany, Spain, and other countries. Any attempt to classify Gothic art by nationality is not in the sphere of an introductory book. To be sure, there were differences between the Gothic of France and that of England and other countries, but the one pervading influence was Christianity, and this gives unity to the general picture.

To most of us, the term Gothic means Gothic cathedral, and the phrase "Gothic cathedral" conjures up a picture of the towers and spires of Chartres, the portals of Amiens or Rheims, or the flying buttresses of Notre-Dame as viewed from across the Seine. These are the well-known features of the Gothic style—the pointed arch, the flying buttress, and the rib vault; but a style is an integral whole, not an aggregate of features. These features were not Gothic inventions; they had evolved through the Romanesque period, and Gothic took the motifs and combined them for a new aesthetic purpose. The pilaster strips on the exterior of the cathedral became flying buttresses; walls were reduced in thickness; the pointed arch was developed to help the builders overcome the difficulties of vaulting; and the apertures in the wall became great glass paintings. Galleries that darkened the interior were done away with, and the emphasis was on lighting and verticality. Thus was evolved a feeling of space and infinity. In the great churches of the past the stability of the structure depended upon weight; in the Gothic church the adjustment of parts produced perfect equilibrium, and the framework of piers, arches, and buttresses was maintained by a system of thrust and counterthrust.

The decisive features of Gothic architecture are the use of light and the aesthetic quality of the structure. Even the windows submit to the pattern of the structure. It is the design of the rib vaults, the shafts, flying buttresses, and pointed arch windows that give the building its aesthetic appeal, and perfection of materials makes the architectural skeleton serve not only the structural stability but also the basic beauty of the edifice. Gothic architecture enlarged its window space until the walls became transparent. Continuous rows of windows allowed the light to permeate the interior until no space remained in darkness, but all glowed with a dim luminous light. This was no happenstance or whim of the builders, but a result of the metaphysical trend of the time. To the thinkers and planners of the twelfth and thirteenth centuries light was the source and essence of all visual beauty. St. Thomas Aquinas, in his *Summa Theologica,* gives his definition of beauty: "For beauty, three things are requisite. In the first place integrity or perfection, for whatsoever things are imperfect by that very fact are ugly; and due proportion or consonance, and again effulgence: so bright coloured objects are said to be beautiful." This aesthetic preference for luminous objects is seen in the gold, precious stones, and glittering objects of liturgical usage. The extensive use of stained glass reflects the same taste that considered light the most noble and least material of natural phenomena and the most direct manifestation of God. Christian theology is centered in the Incarnation and in the Gospel of St. John, which was perceived as light transfiguring the world. In the Gothic Age it became the custom to read the opening verses from the Gospel of St. John, expressing the theology of light at the close of every Mass.

The aesthetics and theology of light reached their highest expression in the Gothic stained-glass window. The colored glass not only tempered the light to give a mystical atmosphere; the designs of the windows gave a panorama of Christian themes, and turned the light of day to Christian purpose. The importance of the stained-glass window in the Gothic church is evidenced by the following quotation, and instructions to those entering a medieval church: "Take Holy Water, adore the Blessed Sacrament, then walk all round the edifice and look at the stained glass."

The Tree of Jesse was a favorite subject in the art of Gothic times. It illustrates Isaiah 11:1-3, and was first used in the eleventh century as an illumination for the Book of Isaiah: "A shoot shall spring forth from the stem of Jesse, and a flower shall blossom at the summit of that shoot and on it shall repose the spirit of the Lord." The early drawings of the Jesse Tree gave a literal illustration. Jesse lies on a couch and holds the Tree at his side. At the top of the Tree is a flower that encloses a dove or an image of the Virgin. Later the Tree of Jesse was a more elaborate composition, and included Prophets and kings from Adam to Christ. The great Tree of Jesse is the window in Chartres Cathedral. The composition is magnificent in its simplicity, and has been the inspiration for many such windows throughout the ages, but none have surpassed it in nobility of conception.

There are two outstanding examples of the Crucifixion in early stained glass. One is in the central window of the *chevet* of the Cathedral of Poitiers. In monumental simplicity of composition, as well as in color, this is perhaps the most beautiful of all stained-glass Crucifixions. Another Crucifixion window is in the church of

Saint-Remi at Rheims. The whole window is a harmony of vibrant blues, reds, greens, yellows, and pale purples, which are in contrast to the pale flesh colors of the figure of Christ. One of the greatest windows from the standpoint of composition and striking color harmony is the well-known Notre-Dame de la Belle-Verrière in the choir of Chartres Cathedral. It dates from the late twelfth century. The hieratic figure of the Virgin robed in blues sits on a throne against a red background; above is a symbolic dove.

When we turn to the sculpture of the Gothic cathedral we find symbolism mingled with nature and realism. The whole thought of the Middle Ages is carved on the portals and columns of the Gothic cathedral. The history of the world, nature, and science were worked into an elaborate theological scheme leading up to and consummated in the divine mystery of Redemption. The Gothic artist drew from Nature herself, which he portrayed with careful observation, yet always with the idea of the world as a symbol. The curling fern frond was made a crocket, and bursting buds and leaves were modeled upon the capitals of columns, while whole branches and vines encircle the cathedral doorways. But in general, religious ornaments tend to show matter bent to express the things of the spirit. Thus, the four symbolical animals of the Evangelists are carved on the tympanums of the portal; the dove of the Holy Ghost, with its symbolical significance, hovers aloft, and the eagle of St. John spreads his wings to support the Gospels at the lectern. The seasons, the signs of the zodiac, and the Vices and Virtues are all carved in lacy stone, but what in the eleventh century was a mixed conglomeration of figures is now organized into compositions of unity and order by means of subordination and concentration upon the dominant figure or idea. Fewer figures are used to tell the story, and the symmetry and rhythm are governed by geometrical rules of harmony. Gestures are restrained; figures do not have the cross-legged contortion of the Romanesque, and there are fewer grotesque monsters. Up to now, architectural sculpture had been in low relief and was decorative in conception. The Gothic sculptured figure steps out from its background and becomes a real statue, not a colonnade. A canopy or tabernacle above and a console below create a spatial shell for the statue, yet the human figure is always subordinated to the architectural order. The portal was the outstanding feature of the Gothic façade, and at these Gothic doorways we find some of the world's greatest sculptured masterpieces. Among the finest portraits of Christ in stone are the portal figures at Notre-Dame, Paris; Chartres Cathedral, and Amiens Cathedral. Though the architectural divisions of the doorway were the same in all Gothic cathedrals, the position of subject matter varied. Portal scenes include the Last Judgment with the figure of Christ, Christ in Majesty, or the Virgin in Majesty. In the rims of the arches are scenes of Hell and Paradise and the Elders of the Apocalypse; in jambs appear the Wise and Foolish Virgins, and on the pillars, Men of the Old Law, the kings and queens of the Old Testament, the Signs of the Zodiac, and the Occupations of the Months.

English Gothic developed along its own lines and was not merely a branch of French Gothic, although Canterbury, the first English Gothic cathedral, was built by a French architect. The typically English feature is the huge square or octagonal tower at the crossing of the transept, and the western end of the cathedral ends in a straight line instead of a curved *chevet*. In English cathedrals the tall perpendicular window replaced the rose window of the French cathedral, and is especially impressive when used with perpendicular tracery, as in the west front of Winchester Cathedral. Also, the façade of the English church was different from that of the French. Instead of sculptured decoration being concentrated at the entrance door, the whole façade was covered with figures in niches, so that it appeared to be a magnificent shrine. This reredos-type façade at Wells Cathedral contains 176 figures, 30 angels, and small reliefs, and includes the Virgin and Child, scenes of the Resurrection, and Christ in Majesty. It is the most important cycle of sculptured figures in England. At Salisbury the façade includes an enlarged version of the French gallery of kings. The west front of Litchfield Cathedral is also covered with tiers of statues, and the rows of niches at Lincoln and Ely cathedrals were planned for figures. But the outstanding sculpture of Lincoln Cathedral is seen in the interior in the magnificent musicians of the Angel Choir.

Germany also had its own version of Gothic, as seen in the great cathedrals of Strasbourg, Freiburg, and Cologne, with their emphasis on vertical lines enhanced by pinnacles and tracery.

Gothic architecture was never at home in Italy, but there are a few outstanding Gothic churches in Italy, such as the early church of San Francisco at Assisi, Santa Maria Novella in Florence, the Cathedral at Milan, and the fourteenth century cathedral at Orvieto with its beautiful sculpture reliefs, frescoes, and goldsmiths' treasures.

In Italy the revival of sculpture brought about by Nicola Pisano was closely tied to architecture. His sculptured pulpits in Pisa and Siena with their columns of green and red granite and panels of scenes of the life of Christ carved in white marble have a sense of depth, individual characterization, and grouping of figures that is Gothic in spirit. The high points of Italian Gothic sculpture were the pulpits of Nicola Pisano, the bas-reliefs on the façade of Orvieto Cathedral attributed to Lorenzo Maitani, the bronze door of the Baptistery at Pisa by Andrea Pisano and finally the Or San Michele in Florence, with its wealth of sculpture by Andrea Orcagna, which formed the transition from Gothic to Renaissance. In these early sculptures there is a combination of ancient Classic sculpture and the observation of nature.

As the Gothic style progressed from early to late Gothic, flamboyant in France or perpendicular in England, it became more sophisticated and more complicated. Geometrical tracery designs changed into flowing ogee patterns, and the stone walls became an intricate network of miniature spires that picked up light and shadow so that the whole structure seemed to move like Monet's sparkling impressionist painting of Rouen Cathedral. Thus encrusted, the lacy network lost the beauty of structural simplicity of the early Gothic; also changing were the medieval mysticism, piety, and ritual that produced the Gothic cathedral and the spirit of Gothic art.

While Gothic architecture and sculpture took the lead in the expression of the Gothic spirit, painting also had an importance not usually recognized. It was the painter who was responsible for the designs of the stained glass, and sculpture and architecture were also painted with bright colors and gilded with gold. Manuscript illumination continued to hold an important place not only in the church and monastery but also under royal patronage. In the thirteenth century handsome Books of Hours, Missals, Psalters, and Bibles were made for wealthy patrons, and these were the work of professional artists. There were schools of illuminators in monastic art centers throughout England in the twelfth century. The most important of these was at Winchester. Psalters, bestiaries, and Apocalypse manuscripts were the most popular forms. Scenes from the life of Christ are painted against brilliant gold or blue or red grounds with small over-all checkered patterns, and are often enclosed in frames resembling the partitions of a stained-glass window. There are distinctive marginal ornaments of beasts, birds, and flowers, and large decorative initials are works of art in themselves, aside from the beauty of the scenes. Two of the most magnificent English illuminated manuscripts of the mid-fourteenth century were the Queen Mary Psalter and the Windmill Psalter.

Similar illuminated manuscripts were painted in France in the thirteenth and fourteenth centuries, such as the Psalter of Blanche of Castile with its medallions of pure sparkling color and simplicity of design. In the Psalter of St. Louis the scenes are set against a cathedral background of rose and lancet windows and pinnacles with flowering crockets that were the forerunner of the Gothic cathedral settings in Flemish paintings. The French miniature of the Gothic Age culminated in the fourteenth century in the work of Jean Pucelle in the famous Belleville Breviary and Petites Heures. The brilliant small paintings by the Limbourgs in the Books of Hours made for Jean, Duke of Berry, in the fifteenth century rank among the great masterpieces of the Middle Ages. In these illuminations we see the architectural settings and interpretations of nature and rich costumes similar to those used by such Gothic painters of Italy as the Lorenzetti. Not to be acquainted with the paintings in these medieval illuminated manuscripts is to miss a rare imaginative and lyric interpretation of Christian art.

Gothic painters also made cartoons for tapestries such as the Apocalypse tapestry at Angers designed by the artist Jean de Bandol in the mid-fourteenth century that is one of the masterpieces of the Gothic Age. It consisted of ninety pictures, of which seventy exist. Its aesthetic effect is due to simplicity of line and form, strong contrasts of values, and a small range of color with strong blue and red predominating. Gothic painting also includes altarpieces, panels, diptychs, and frescoes. There were panel paintings on wood and triptychs and diptychs for altarpieces. Large painted wooden crosses to hang on the iconostasis or on the Triumphal Arch were made particularly in Italy and Spain. These were surrounded by small panels with the stories of the Passion.

With the shifting of emphasis from the cathedral, that is, from architecture to painting, the leadership in Gothic art went from France to Flanders. Here the love and exaltation of the Gothic Te Deum was prolonged by Flemish artists. This idealistic art steeped in myths and stories from the "Golden Legend" prospered under royal sponsorship in the art centers of Bruges and Tournai from the middle of the fourteenth century. Realism combines with mysticism. Scenes of the Annunciation and the Madonna with saints and donors are placed against a background of everyday life—the interior of a Gothic or Romanesque church or the domesticity of a house of a Flemish burgher. Even such lofty and nobly conceived works as van Eyck's "The Adoration of the Lamb" and "The Nativity" of the Master of Flémalle have background settings of the spires and belfries of Bruges or Tournai and the green meadows and winding roads of the Flemish countryside. Space is suggested by color contrasts—strong warm colors of the foreground, warm and cool in the middle distance, and cool blue greens in the distance. Yet this pictorial reality is handled with such sincerity and freshness that the commonplace becomes monumental and dignified. These pictures are peaceful and quiet, and they satisfied the longings of the hearts of the people of the fifteenth century. But their spiritual message is hard for us to understand today unless we too become as children, and accept them with faith. A study of their intricate symbolism and iconography will increase our enjoyment, and is especially necessary for a full understanding of them.

The Mérode Altarpiece, a scene of the Annunciation, which was acquired by the Cloisters of the Metropolitan Museum in 1957, is an example of interwoven realism and symbolism. The scene of the center panel shows the angel and the Virgin in an ordinary Flemish interior. The mood of the scene is quiet and unassuming but a supernatural light fills the room and the work breathes a sanctity that moves one to silence and awe. Each object of daily usage in the picture has been painted with devotion and reverence and is a part of the intricate symbolism that gave a theological concept to all familiar objects. In the well-known "Adoration of the Lamb," the Ghent Altarpiece by the van Eycks, symbolism and reality combine in expressing the theme of the Redemption through the Blood of the Lamb.

Rogier van der Weyden relates his pictures more closely with the Middle Ages. Church interiors are used as settings, and backgrounds have an abstract gold backdrop or a hung drapery as in the Crucifixion in Philadelphia. In this diptych the tall sculptural forms are almost abstract, yet they express strong emotion and spiritual distress not connected with individual forms. Similarly, in the famous "Descent from the Cross" in the Prado, Madrid, the sculpture-like form, the plastic treatment of the draperies, the lines of the composition, and the expression of intense emotion tell the dramatic story against a flat gold background without realistic detail or symbolism.

Dirk Bouts, Hugo van der Goes, Hans Memling, and Gerard David carried on the tradition that had been established by the great Flemish masters of the early fifteenth century. Dirk Bouts' altarpiece, "The Last Supper," in St. Peters, Louvain, is one of the great works of Flemish art. It depicts the institution of the Eucharist, and the four lateral panels show incidents of the Old Testament foreshadowing the Last Supper. The shadow of Protestantism gives a new, matter-of-fact conception to the scene. Stress is on the human aspect of the scene and on the individuality of man.

Jerome Bosch's fantastic and original iconography and strange world of imaginary forms seem monstrous and terrifying, yet recent research has revealed Bosch's connection with the late medieval interpretation of the Bible and the popular art forms of his era. The underlying theme of Bosch's subject matter deals with the moral life, the meaning of human existence, and man's relation to the world around him. Though all his subjects are religious, he does not follow tradition, but rather the writings of fourteenth and fifteenth century mystics, which are expressed in symbols of color, number, and name mingled with the lore of alchemy and magic. His world is that of the inner man, mental and immaterial. From the standpoint of the Church and Christian art, Bosch has a message, and in these days of uninhibited and outspoken frankness we may be able to overlook the lewd symbolism and accept the aesthetic beauty of Bosch's color and composition and the splendor of his landscapes, and, with guided interpretation, understand the spiritual depth of his message.

Also medieval in spirit were the deeply religious paintings produced in Provence, France, in the fifteenth century. In the well known "Villeneuve Pietà" in the Louvre, huge monumental figures with passionate but restrained emotions are placed against a flat gold background with the towers and domes of a Jerusalem in the distance. Less well known is the "Coronation of the Virgin" in the Hospice of Villeneuve-les-Avignon by Enguerrand Charonton. According to tradition the subject matter is arranged on three horizontal planes—the celestial above, the earthy in the center, and Hell and Purgatory below. Nicolas Froment's decorative triptych "The Burning Bush," in the Cathedral of Saint-Sauveur, Aix-en-Provence, and "The Nativity" of the Master of Moulins carry on the medieval tradition that culminates in the work of Jean Fouquet, a painter and illuminator of Books of Hours that are examples of the best illumination of the fifteenth century.

Before 1500, painting in Germany was secondary to architecture and wood carving. Primitive schools of painting existed in various parts of Germany, and although they were influenced by the art of other countries, they were sometimes characterized by a native German mysticism and fantastic imagination that was to develop in German art of the next century. At other times paintings showed a realism and modern spirit, as is seen in the work of Conrad Witz and Martin Schongauer, who did memorable work before the great period of Dürer, Cranach, Grünewald, and Holbein.

While the Gothic painters in northern Europe were mainly concerned with stained glass, manuscripts, tapestries, and altarpieces, in Italy church decoration relied on the fresco as it had down through the ages, and there is an unbroken sequence of Christian art in Italian fresco painting. Though the feeling of the Italian Gothic harks back to early Christianity, to naïve faith and piety, it also breathes a note of humanism through the influence of the kindly personal Christianity of St. Francis. The paintings that reflect this spirit are at the same time modestly and devotedly Christian in theme and in spirit but sensuously beautiful with life-enhancing color and gold. Kindness, charity, and compassion, simplicity and calm are expressed in line and color through the incidents and imagery. The message of this art transforms through devotion and the belief that all beautiful things were eloquent of the divine order. Faces and figures have a human grace and sweetness, and their attitudes express devotion. The Madonna becomes a Mother, and in the scenes of the Passion takes on some of the pathos of suffering. Interpreters of this spirit were the Sienese painters Duccio, Simone Martini, Sassetta and, foremost of all, Giotto.

Giotto's original and dramatic compositions set his work apart from the main stream of Gothic painting, but on the spiritual plane there is a kinship. Giotto rejected the dead weight of tradition and reshaped to his own ends that which was vital and significant for his age; while there still remains much that is medieval, Giotto's painting marks the dawn of the Italian Renaissance. In his pictures of the life of St. Francis the compositions are unified and there is a natural relation between figures, architecture, landscape, and light that creates a sense of space. His figures have a tactile quality that brings us in contact with them, and the simplicity of their natural gestures creates a solemnity befitting the subject matter. Giotto was concerned with the social implications of Christ's teachings. His illustrations of the stories of the Christian Faith conceal no hidden spiritual meanings, but are preserved as facts. By giving the semblance of daily life to Christian thought, Giotto emphasized one of the universal aspects of Christianity, and his pictures have meaning for Christians today even as they did in his own age.

Fra Angelico worked fifty years after the death of Giotto, but he carries on the Franciscan spirit. His painting is medieval in its manner, and in its expression of adoration, ecstasy, and heavenly glory, belongs to the Gothic Age. Fra Angelico's content is gentle and sweet; he forgets the violence and agony of the Christian story. He seeks to recapture the perfect forms of things as God intended them to be, and for this he employs a fusion of form, light, and radiant, luminous color. His Annunciations possess a sense of mystery, and his Crucifixions are mystical representations, not narrative scenes. His landscapes express idyllic quietude, suggesting psalms, hymns, and spiritual songs, and his interpretations of religious scenes are devout expressions of Christianity closely akin to that indefinable beauty of holiness.

In addition to the fine arts of architecture, sculpture, and painting the Gothic period also excelled in the lesser arts of metalwork and ivory carving. There are beautiful ivories with scenes of the Passion set within frames of Gothic arches. Ivory bookbindings are studded with jewels and medallions of colorful enamels. Bishop's staffs and croziers were carved of ivory. Beautiful candlesticks, candelabra, chalices, and similar articles of liturgical usage were made of gold, silver, and other metals chased with Gothic tracery and often studded with precious jewels. In the Gothic period these objects of liturgical usage took on more form. They became as graceful and slender as the lines of the architecture. The motifs of design included Gothic tracery, and in the late Gothic period the patterns of gilt tracery became lacelike. Gothic niches of ivory and metalwork were filled with figures similar to those in the stonework of the churches.

Early croziers were of a simple form similar to a shepherd's staff. Next they take on the suggestion of a budding branch that sometimes blooms forth with naturally formed leaves. Those covered with gold and enamelwork have a figure such as the Lamb, St. George and Dragon, an angel and the Virgin of the Annunciation, or a Virgin and Child in the circle of the crozier head. Late Gothic crozier heads often enclosed a figure set in a Gothic niche or the replica of a Gothic church. Censers were usually modeled in the form of churches, the early ones Byzantine, then following the styles of Gothic and Renaissance architecture. Candlesticks of enamel and silver-gilt and crystal and silver-gilt were of fine proportion and simple design. Elaborate candelabra embossed and sculptured with figures and decorative leaf and flower designs were also made. Shrines by twelfth and thirteenth century German goldsmiths are masterpieces. But these are only a presage of the glory that was to come with the refinement of the work of the Renaissance goldsmith.

We have made no attempt to bind the Gothic period by exact dates, for even the experts cannot agree. Gothic art in its highest expression is an art of the cathedral. Everything is in some way connected with the cathedral, and has religious significance. The illuminated manuscripts, the statues, the stained glass and the articles of religious use are expositions of medieval Christian faith. Paintings such as van Eyck's Madonnas have a cathedral background; the scenes on ivory carvings are set against Gothic façades; and even the composition of paintings and statues is arranged about a center like the columns around a center shaft in the Gothic cathedral. Owing to this concentration of spiritual purpose, Gothic art stands out as one of the greatest expressions of the ideals of Christian religion. Because of its human qualities it has an appeal and message for us today where earlier Christian art, no matter how intense its fervor or how great its expression, may fail to communicate its message.

CHAPTER VII

ART AND ARCHITECTURE OF THE RENAISSANCE

I shall define Beauty to be harmony of all the parts in whatsoever subject it appears, fitted together with such proportion and connection that nothing could be added, diminished or altered.

—ALBERTI

For those of us who received our art education before the turn of the midcentury, the Renaissance, particularly in Italy, was pictured as a sentimental journey. We visited Florence where we saw Fra Angelico's frescoes at San Marco and those of Giotto at Santa Croce; we saw Brunelleschi's Pazzi Chapel with its majolica decorations by Luca della Robbia; San Lorenzo with frescoes by Verrocchio; and the Or San Michele with sculpture by Verrocchio, Donatello, and others as well known; then the Duomo, Baptistery, and Campanile—the dome Brunelleschi's, the Campanile Giotto's, and the picturesque bronze "Doors of Paradise" by Ghiberti.

But the Renaissance is more than a Cook's tour. For art, the Renaissance meant the change in architecture, painting, and sculpture brought about by the new spirit of Humanism and the rediscovery of the antique. Renaissance art borrowed the forms and setting of antiquity and modified them with a new spirit. The first period of the Renaissance is marked by the fusion of the forms of the Middle Ages and those of antiquity, and is a period of transition. Indeed, the dawn of the Renaissance is indistinguishable from the twilight of the Gothic, for the breath of Humanism was in the Gothic cathedral and in the paintings of Giotto, but it was a Humanism of the spirit, while the Humanism of the Renaissance was fleshy and realistic. The Gothic delight in nature was made to serve God, but the Renaissance artist loved nature for itself. The absorption in the physical world is seen in the paintings of the van Eycks and the school of the Netherlands and in the paintings of

Filippo Lippi and Botticelli in Italy, yet they painted with Christian purpose and with the intent of serving the Church. However, the spiritual element was materialized, and religious emotions mingled with aesthetic charm and sensuous beauty to give the Renaissance contribution to Christian Art.

The Renaissance was also an age of advance in science and mathematics, of expansion in space, and of the discovery of new countries. This interest and expansion in space was also the concern of Renaissance artists who introduced perspective and the third dimension. By a new technique of vision Brunelleschi and Donatello related solid objects to each other and to the area about them in a way that was convincing to the mind and to the eye and which gave a third dimension and an illusion of deep space. This new concept of space changed the whole conception of art. In Byzantine and medieval art a hierarchical perspective was used that scaled the size of figures to their ritual or psychological importance. An optical perspective was the innovation of Giotto, who saw the world from an individual viewpoint. Leonardo da Vinci employed an atmospheric perspective that clothed the distance in a haze. Atmospheric effects were also used by the sculptors Donatello and Desiderio da Settignano, who carved planes in half-relief to give contrast and distance. Warm advancing colors and cool receding colors as used by Flemish painters also gave an effect of perspective. However, we usually think of perspective as the vanishing-point or "railroad track" perspective where objects arranged on lines of convergence diminish as they approach the vanishing point. This type of perspective was new with the Renaissance. Geometric forms such as buildings and archways were incorporated into pictures, and the relation between the perspective of the buildings and the figures united the design with the idea of the picture. The composition of Raphael's "The School of Athens," with the principal figures set in the receding archways, and Leonardo da Vinci's "The Last Supper," with the figure of Christ set at the point where the lines of architectural perspective converge, are examples of perspective employed to unify the composition of a picture. But Renaissance aesthetic space is not simply projection; it is composition within three dimensions composed from a fixed point of view. By creating this illusion of space, the painter humanized space so that it heightens our feeling of well-being. Through fine proportion Renaissance art achieves a single vision of aesthetic harmony and unity. Forms become significant because they have aesthetic beauty rather than moral, religious, or naturalistic values.

In its broadest sense the Renaissance represented the expansion and attainment of freedom of the human spirit. In art there was a freedom of expression in the movement of figures and their natural relationship to one another in a unified representation seen from a single point of view. Until Renaissance times the subject matter of art had been presented in a sequence of scenes like a panorama; in contrast, Renaissance works of art have unity and homogeneity. This new freedom and new outlook struck a blow at the dogma, authority, and scholasticism that controlled the Christian art of the Middle Ages, and some of the legends and symbolism of medieval Christianity crumbled in the light of a new age. Men began to look around at the beauties of nature, and what they saw was good. They observed the human body not as a stiff, lifeless form, but as something beautiful and noble in itself. Giotto and Duccio and their followers, with the help of the Franciscan spirit, had begun to see the world in this new light, but they were a century ahead.

Renaissance frescoes and altar paintings took another step toward the humanizing of Christian art. The Madonna and Child changed from symbols to human beings, and the episodes of the Bible were dramatized. Gradually the attention drifted from the dogma and history of the Church to the beauty of the work of art. Emancipating itself from ecclesiastical authority, art glorified the majesty and splendor of the human body, and in the High Renaissance created religious subjects in which there is nothing mystical or devotional beyond humanity. Finally a spirit alien to Christianity turned to paganism, and portrayed satyrs, Pan, and legends of classic mythology; and art delighted in beauty for its own sake.

Brunelleschi, Donatello, and Masaccio were the torchbearers of the Italian Renaissance, and Florence was the city of enlightenment in the fifteenth century. Brunelleschi's famous dome of the Duomo in Florence initiated the Renaissance style of architecture. The Gothic style had been created for the Church, but the Renaissance was created for the Medici and the rich merchants of Florence. The centrally planned Renaissance church was designed, not for infinity but for its aesthetic appeal, and the craving for beauty was given preference over the necessities of the service. The purpose of the plan of the medieval church, both Romanesque and Gothic, had been to lead the attention toward the altar by progressive steps. In a centralized building, whether circular or in the form of a Greek cross, no such movement is possible. Man stands in one place enjoying the beauty, not pressing toward the infinite, for "he" is the center of this beauty. This relationship characterizes the attitude of Humanism, and thus relates the centralized church to Renaissance man, who did want to be reminded of infinity, but wanted an architecture to eternalize the present. The basilica in the shape of the Latin cross, representing Christ crucified, was replaced by the form of the Greek cross and square churches with central domes. The Roman triumphal arch was adapted as the façade of the Renaissance Church, and colonnades held large sculptural figures. In the interior there was splendor of materials, but purity and simplicity were sought in the use of colors, with white preferred. The dome painted with stars has a cosmic significance, and the circle produces a soothing effect. The walls are reestablished and enlivened and divided by decorative elements such as moldings, friezes, and pilasters. This finding again of the proper function of the wall and the mastery of space and the third dimension was the problem of the Renaissance architect.

Sculpture of the early Renaissance was related to architecture and was in the form of reliefs for church façades, bronze doors, pulpits, figures to fit architectural niches, tabernacles, or for monumental tombs. Such objects of liturgical usage as altars, Paschal candlesticks, crosses, and chalices were usually the work of sculptor-goldsmiths.

Siena was the center of the goldsmith's craft until the fifteenth century, when Florence gained prominence, but there were also excellent goldsmiths in other Italian towns such as Perugia and Bologna, and north of the Alps, in Germany. The acme of perfection of the goldsmith's craft was the silver-gilt altar frontal with its chased and embossed scenes of the life of Christ in a pattern of rectangles or squares. The famous baptistery altar frontal in the Museo Opera del Duomo, Florence, with sculptured scenes by Pollaiuolo and Verrocchio, was made in the fourteenth century. Florence continued to be the center for goldsmiths' work well into the sixteenth century, although there were also fine goldsmiths in Germany, Flanders, and France, as well as England and Spain.

Renaissance reliquaries are lantern-shape, with domes, rounded arches, and Renaissance pediments. Reliquaries were also made in the form of arms, heads, and busts and sometimes were portraits of actual persons. Crosses of the Middle Ages had sculptured figures set in medallions. Altar crosses of enamel were set in bases of bronze or rock crystal. The famous Cross of the Pisans in Lucca Cathedral has a silver-gilt sculptured figure of Christ set among lilies, and the Cross of the Baptistery Altar in the Museo del Duomo, in Florence, has sculptured figures by the artist Pollaiuolo.

In 1401 three great sculptors, Brunelleschi, Ghiberti, and della Quercia, were among those who competed in the contest for the design of the bronze doors of the Baptistery in Florence. The contest was won by Ghiberti. His doors depict scenes from the Bible in episodes including the Annunciation, Baptism, Agony in the Garden, Crucifixion, and Resurrection. Ghiberti later did another set of doors for the Baptistery known as the "Gates of Paradise." The episodes on these doors were set in rectangular compositions of larger scope, including such subjects as the Creation. In these, Ghiberti used the old iconography but created new concepts of space, movement, and composition that influenced not only other sculptors but painters as well. Andrea Pisano, della Quercia, Luca della Robbia, and Donatello also designed bronze doors with Biblical scenes.

In order to embody the ideas of Christianity, art had to be concerned more with expression than with form, and although this is the special sphere of painting, sculpture attempted to follow, and used facial expressions and drapery in an effort to express Christian emotions. Donatello's reliefs on the doors of the Old Sacristy in San Lorenzo show originality and inventiveness. Instead of narrative scenes he broke away from the set tradition, and pictures saints, two to a panel, and by eloquent gesture and deportment he related the figures. His figures of Prophets for the Campanile in Florence present the Biblical characters as real persons with a dramatic liveliness. One meditates, another reads, another moves as to speak, while the last is exclaiming with parted lips. Antonio Rossellino, Mino da Fiésole, and Settignano confined themselves to tranquil beauty and an idyllic, poetic expression. When Donatello designed his Cantoria, or choir balcony, for the Duomo in Florence, another sculptor, Luca della Robbia, was commissioned to design the opposite Cantoria. Della Robbia's memory has been cheapened by

Coptic bearded saint in orant attitude. Limestone, sixth or seventh century. *Dumbarton Oaks Collection.*

Apse mosaic in St. Pudenziana, Rome. Christ and the Apostles, with jeweled cross and symbols of Evangelists in background. Fifth century. *Photo Alinari.*

PLATE II

Opposite: The Good Shepherd Sarcophagus, Lateran Museum, Rome. Third century. *Photo Anderson, Rome.*

The colonnaded Sarcophagus of Junius Bassus, A.D. 359, in the Vatican Crypt, shows scenes from the Old and New Testaments, including Apollonic Christ, enthroned (*top center*), journey to Jerusalem (*bottom center*), Adam and Eve, and Daniel. *Photo Anderson, Rome.*

Opposite: Nave mosaic, "The Hospitality of Abraham," in St. Maria Maggiore, Rome, is a blending of the picturesque art of Alexandria and the narrative art of Rome. Fourth century. *Photo Alinari.*

PLATE III

Basilica of St. Apollinare in Classe, Ravenna. Mosaic on arch is of Christ with symbols of the Evangelists. The apse mosaic shows a large cross on a ground of stars, a symbolic Transfiguration with Moses and Elias and Apostles as lambs. Below are St. Apollinaris and a procession of lambs. *Photo Alinari.*

The Moggio Pyxis of Daniel in the lions' den. Ivory, Egypt, sixth century. *Dumbarton Oaks Collection.*

Crucifixion panel from doors of St. Sabina, Rome, ca. 430. A bearded Christ stands in an attitude of prayer, with His hands nailed to blocks. *Photo Anderson, Rome.*

PLATE VI

In the apse of the Cathedral Monreale, Sicily, are shown Christ Pantocrator, with the Virgin enthroned, angels and saints below. *Photo Alinari.*

The Riha Paten of silver repoussé and gilt, showing the communion of the Apostles. Syria, sixth century. *Dumbarton Oaks Collection.*

Reliquary casket of ivory, Museo Civico, Brescia. From the top: portrait heads; story of Jonah and the whale; Christ healing the woman with issue; reading in the synagogue; Christ as the Good Shepherd; Susanna and the elders. *Photo Anderson, Rome.*

PLATE VIII

A Byzantine silver chalice, sixth century. Two crosses and four saints are framed in an arcade. The knob is a leaf design; the foot is fluted. *Walters Art Gallery, Baltimore.*

Byzantine enamels of the eleventh century: St. John the Evangelist above and St. Luke below. *Metropolitan Museum of Art, Gift of J. Pierpont Morgan.*

Christ enthroned, from the Book of Kells, Trinity College, Dublin, Ireland, ninth century. The robes of the figure of Christ repeat the curves of the arabesque patterns. *Photo Green Studio, Dublin.*

PLATE XI

Center: St. John the Baptist, with St. Philip and St. Stephen above, St. Andrew and St. Thomas below. Byzantine pierced ivory relief, tenth century. *Victoria and Albert Museum, London.*

A ninth century Nativity scene on ivory from a cover of the Gospels. *Victoria and Albert Museum, London.*

Abbey church of St. Maria di Pomposa (800–1026) shows the austerity of early Lombard architecture with simple colonnade ornament and earliest type of rose window. *Photo Alinari.*

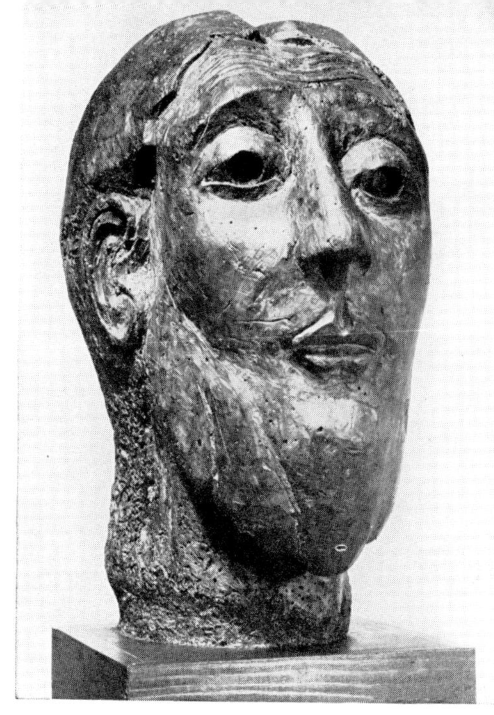

Head of Christ. Wood sculpture, Tongres, Belgium, twelfth century.
A.C.L., Bruxelles.

Tympanum of the Last Judgment at Beaulieu, France. *Archives Photographiques.*

St. Gavin-sur-Gartempe: the great height and massive columns give a solemnity that is echoed in the wall and ceiling paintings depicting scenes from the Old Testament and from Revelation. Twelfth century. *Archives Photographiques.*

Christ and the Apostles, from the portal between the narthex and the nave, Vézelay, France. Early twelfth century. *Archives Photographiques.*

Cathedral at Pisa: detail of bronze doors, twelfth century. Upper panels show Solomon's Judgment and the Baptism of Christ; in the lower panels are the Nativity and the Journey of the Wise Men. *Photo Alinari.*

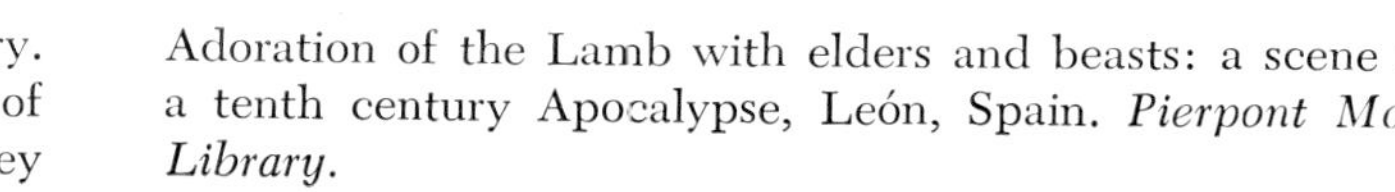

Adoration of the Lamb with elders and beasts: a scene from a tenth century Apocalypse, León, Spain. *Pierpont Morgan Library.*

Royal Portal, Chartres: Christ in Majesty with symbols of the Evangelists. *Archives Photographiques.*

The Adoration of the Magi, whalebone, English, twelfth century. The composition gives prominence to the Virgin and Child first by means of size and then by the archway over the large head of the Virgin as a halo. A niche is formed for the Child by the lines of the Virgin's cloak. The Virgin's face is smooth in contrast to the intricate carving of the rest of the surfaces. *Victoria and Albert Museum, London.*

the numerous reproductions of his majolica plaques, but many of his Madonnas and figures of Prophets have distinction.

However, painting was the most expressive medium for the ideals of the Renaissance. The painter's imagination dramatized the Biblical scenes and by means of life-enhancing beauty quickened the sacred images. Yet underlying all else was the fact that in Christianity the moral and spiritual values were of utmost importance. The expression of these qualities did not require physical perfection, but an ideal world that was related to the invisible. In order to make the human body interpret the symbol of the soul and to express pain and passion, painting had to suggest more than it depicted—this by means of aesthetic qualities. The psychological use of line could suggest infinity by means of tall vertical lines, rhythm and grace by the curve, and peace and tranquillity with horizontal lines. Color could also be used to express moods of the soul, and aesthetically related spaces could suggest the mystery of the unknown, while landscape could be made to correspond and accentuate the mood and feeling of the idea of such noble subjects as the Crucifixion and the Resurrection.

Masaccio, like Donatello, cut loose from tradition and became the first great painter of the Italian Renaissance. The plastic quality of his massive immobile figures relates his painting to architecture. His solemn figures are painted in low-keyed somber colors that give them a heroic style and an elemental link with all mankind. Although Masaccio's paintings are deeply religious, he locates his themes on earth, in the heart of reality, as though to remind the beholder that the spiritual significance of the scene is constantly renewed in the Christian's daily life; and so great are his tactile values that we feel the impact of the message. But although Masaccio and Donatello represented the classic statuesque style of the fifteenth century, many artists working at the same time still followed the Gothic tradition.

In a period where artists and their works fill not only the churches but also the halls of the great guilds and spiritual fraternities, it is difficult to select those to be mentioned here. However, the purpose of our thesis narrows our choice to the artists who have most successfully expressed the religious theme rather than artists who may be significant in the development of the science of painting or sculpture. Thus, instead of calling to special attention the works of such great painters as Uccello, whose chief interest is perspective, or Ghirlandajo, who fills his religious pictures with genre, we mention Castagno, who paints a "Last Supper" with powerful simplicity even though his figures seem wooden as compared to Masaccio's. The pious paintings of Fra Filippo Lippi have gained popularity with Church people, but Lippi essentially is interested in the world about him—the architecture, the landscape, the appealing women, and the playful children—and his effort to express such realities interferes with his creative conception.

Piero della Francesca places statuesque, heroic figures majestic as marble columns against backgrounds of architecture or barren landscape. His interest is in pure aesthetics, but so great is his composition and so impelling are his tactile values that his interpretations of the religious scene are Christian in the highest sense. His figures of Christ in "The Baptism of Christ" and "The Resurrection" have dignity, majesty, and calm. The Risen Christ is an awesome figure against the luminous gray sky of dawn and a few cypress and plane trees. The solemn frontal figure with piercing eyes dominates the scene and becomes a sacred image that interprets the importance of the moment and gives us a belief in the Mystery.

Botticelli, like Fra Filippo Lippi, has long been a popular favorite because of his seemingly sweet and sentimental Madonnas and the surface beauty of his painting. Yet his painting has depth and mysticism and a beauty of line that moves in melodic rhythms akin to music and poetry. It is this linear movement that stimulates our imagination and gives us pleasure. Botticelli's Madonnas, set within a circle and built up on curved arcs and crescents, have the organic structure of a budding flower, and give a mysterious psychological effect. His later works have an austere mysticism and reflect the religious conflicts of the age. Such compositions as "The Pietà" and "The Last Communion of St. Jerome" are in a different mood, and seem to be a protest against the neopaganism of the Renaissance.

One of the greatest painters of the fifteenth century was Andrea Mantegna, of the Venetian-Paduan School, but he used such subjects as the Ascension and Crucifixion as occasions for a reproduction of the antique world rather than for the expression of Christian feeling. In "The Agony in the Garden" the beautiful composition of stony crags with the city of Rome in the distance creates a pleasure-giving beauty. In contrast, the similar composition by Giovanni Bellini has a deep spiritual quality, and by making our Lord the prominent feature relates more nearly to the text of the Bible in which Christ's prayer and the divine answer make it one of the most solemn scenes of the New Testament. In his "Pietà" Bellini makes dramatic use of lighting, and the luminous clouds correspond to the mood of despair and hopelessness of the human figures. The clouds and the facial expression are also in accord in "Christ Blessing," and Bellini's early Madonnas have a remote gaze that expresses piety and the profound sentiments of religious feeling. Without any dramatic aids to devotion, Bellini's "Transfiguration" expresses solemn emotion and awe.

Perugino, the teacher of Raphael, also used backgrounds of nature and architecture as an aid in expressing his spiritual mood of quiet worship. The serene beauty of Classical architecture and the beauty of archways repeated by circles of angels' heads gives spiritual and aesthetic feeling to his Annunciations and Madonnas, while the musical rhythm of space in the calm landscape gives a peaceful assurance to Perugino's well-known "Crucifixion with Saints."

In the sixteenth century, under the patronage of the popes, Rome became the art center of the Christian world. This art of the High Renaissance was classic, formal, disciplined, solemn, and majestic, and corresponded to the formal code of society and religion of the time. There are no tears or grimaces of pain. Christ is no longer a suffering martyr; He again becomes a heavenly King. The Virgin neither weeps nor wrings her hands, but reveals calmness of bearing. Bible characters are represented as physical personalities in the form of the sixteenth century ideal of a heroic, dignified, courtly person with elegant physical beauty. Formal compositions based on the circle and triangle organize figures with concentration and subordination, and the heavenly sphere in Christian art is represented not by the supernatural but by creating distance between the human and the divine. The most famous painters of the High Renaissance, Leonardo da Vinci, Raphael, Titian, Michelangelo, and Correggio expressed these characteristics.

Leonardo da Vinci's perfected expressions of tactile values and atmospheric effects, together with his insight and interpretation of subject matter, give his paintings a universal appeal. In "The Last Supper" he retained the tranquillity of the scene and the majesty of the figure of Christ, but at the same time humanized the subject and added drama and an insight into the spiritual meaning. To this feeling for the beauty and significance of the scene, in the painting "The Virgin of the Rocks" are added mystery, awe, and perfection of composition that give pleasure as the eye follows lines and forms. His sense of form was always subordinate to the expression of spiritual meaning.

"Raphael," to quote Berenson, "was a great illustrator and a great space-composer." We are drawn to the paintings of Raphael, as to those of Perugino and Leonardo da Vinci, because of the serene beauty of the figures and the hushed quiet of the landscape setting; but subconsciously we are also affected by the beauty of the composition in space that takes us out of ourselves and gives us far horizons and open vistas identified with the infinite. However, many of Raphael's paintings, particularly his Madonnas, such as "The Madonna of the Chair" and the "Sistine Madonna," have become so familiar and cheapened by poor reproductions that we can no longer look at them with any sense of art appreciation. If, instead, we look at the less-familiar "Alba Madonna" in the National Gallery of Art, with its soulful Mother enthroned against the landscape, we shall appreciate anew the fluid quality of his painting and the beautiful curves of his composition in space that give the feeling of spirituality.

Raphael's majestic religious style is illustrated in such compositions as the "Disputa" and the "Mass of Bolsena." The "Mass of Bolsena" illustrates a miracle that convinces a doubting priest and symbolizes the triumph of the popes over the cardinals. Thus it is a historic picture of the Church and not of the Bible. In contrast, one of Raphael's most profound religious pictures is "The Transfiguration." This painting is a devotional interpretation, a revelation of earthly suffering as shown in the scene in the foreground, and of spiritual faith as revealed in the radiant figure of Christ in mid-air between Elijah and Moses. Yet the perfection of Raphael was the beginning of the dullness that characterizes sacred art and makes it empty and lacking in vitality.

The height of the splendor and luxury of the Venetians is consummated in the glow of Titian's color. We see it in the rich velvets and brocades of his portraits or in the garden backgrounds where the world of beauty serves as a frame for his great religious paintings. Titian's "The Assumption of the Virgin" was painted within a few years of Raphael's "The Transfiguration." The paintings are similar in composition, with a foreground scene of life on earth and a celestial scene above. Here the grandeur, dignity, and beauty of Christian art give its message to us in Titian's harmony of light and shade and luminous color. "The Tribute Money," with its sublime portrait of Christ, and "The Entombment," in the Louvre, are well known but still impressive; but whatever Titian was painting, beauty of color harmony was always his theme. "The ideal that life can be enriched through art," wrote Max Dvorak, "took its rise with Titian."

The art of the High Renaissance reached its peak with Michelangelo. As an architect he planned the Gesú Church and the dome of St. Peter's. But the essence of Michelangelo's genius is revealed in his early sculpture, such as the marble "Pietà." The same classic beauty is in the face of the "Madonna and Child" at Bruges. In "David" Michelangelo took on a more heroic Classic style that climbs to great strength, elemental power, and plastic vitality in the figures of the Medici Tombs and the great Moses on the tomb of Julius II who stands as the symbol of the righteous anger of a man with a high mission. Fully to understand the art of Michelangelo and the great religious fervor of his inspiration, we must read his own words: "True artistic inspiration is not derived from the material world. The visible universe has value only in reflecting the divine idea. When external beauty penetrates into the soul by the mortal eye it is transformed into the heart's image and the outward image is transcended into universal form due to the divine nature of the soul."

In Michelangelo's painting in the Sistine Chapel it is already evident that the grand style of the Renaissance is breaking up, and anti-Classical tendencies, such as disintegration of space and structural unity, are apparent. Composition is disturbed and rules of proportion and perspective are defied, and the artist manipulates the design to satisfy his own needs of expression. In this he anticipated the mannerist artists who followed, and especially the work of Tintoretto. In addition, such painting is closely allied to the expressionism of today, and was perhaps brought about by similar causes of broken world patterns and conflicts. For into the closed circle of the Renaissance came schisms, Luther's burning of the papal bull in 1520, and the sacking of Rome in 1527. Everywhere people became aware that the otherworldliness and inner spirituality of the Christian Faith were lost, and there was a strong desire to restore it by a new deepening of religious life. Against this turbulent background Michelangelo and other sensitive artists with strong belief in the Christian Faith sought to interpret the Gospels and to keep alive the dying mystical content of Christian emotion.

In the Sistine Chapel paintings Michelangelo gives his philosophical conception of human existence and expresses the tragedy of the human soul. The depth of his conception and the breadth of his vision make this ceiling great art. He changes the iconography of Bible scenes by going back to the Biblical source rather than following tradition. On ceilings of churches Heaven was usually represented by a blue sky and stars, but Michelangelo populates Heaven with figures and expressive forms of God. These figures of God become more and more celestial as they proceed in various episodes of creation from the entrance of the chapel to the altar. The swelling masses of the huge figures transcend reality and are creatures of a new world with divine origins. In 1535 Michelangelo was commissioned to paint "The Last Judgment" over the altar at the end of the chapel. This scene is presented with dramatic force and apocalyptic intensity, and expresses Michelangelo's mystical faith and the inner conflict of his soul.

Tintoretto also deviated from the norm that the Renaissance considered golden. By means of interrelated light, space, and movement, he opens up a new visual world. He abandons the central arrangement of composition and breaks up form and color with light so that all becomes an expressive rhythmical movement that takes on a life of its own. Color is used psychologically—subdued or heavy —according to the subject. But lighting was the key to his emotional effect. He arbitrarily places light and shade where he wants them. In "The Crucifixion" in San Rocco, Venice, the spiritual impact of the picture is expressed by means of light. It is an unnatural light neither indoors nor outdoors, neither daylight nor dark, but an ominous twilight. In grandeur of conception and depth of understanding, the composition is one of the greatest of Christian Crucifixions. The center group of figures builds up a triangle that points toward the Cross, and the ladder leads the eye to the figure of Christ centered in dramatic light. Hundreds of figures go about their business of setting up the other crosses or idly watching the scene, but this only adds to the pathos.

Dürer also lived amid the strife, uncertainty, and the clash of religion in sixteenth century Germany. There were heavenly signs —meteors and comets, tales of nuns' stigmata and holy wafers stained with a cross of blood. Somewhere between these primitive fears and mystical visions and the Lutheran certitude of Faith lies Dürer's religious art. His art has the traditional solemnity and intellectual structure prescribed by the Roman Catholic Church, yet in his drawings and prints he presents the world of the Reformation. But although his art is of the Reformation period, it is not Protestant nor is it servant to any particular creed. Dürer presents no new subjects for Christian iconography, but he treats the old themes with warmth, passion, humanity, and originality. As in early Christian art, the narration of the episode becomes of first importance, and to interpret the soul Dürer uses all the realism at his command. Within the pattern of Biblical story, Dürer expresses worship, ecstasy, silent adoration, supplication, thanksgiving, and confession by means of expressive gestures that vary according to the depth of spiritual feeling. His pictures have universal appeal because they are understood by all.

The German mysticism with its medieval elements and irrational and fantastic characteristics noted in Dürer and in the religious paintings of Schongauer, Hans Baldung (Grien), Rueland Frueauf, and Stephan Lochner, culminated in the vehement paintings of Grünewald. The combination of antique and everyday realism, the mixture of the invisible and the tangible, and the intensity of emotion and ecstatic fervor set Grünewald apart and make his pictures unique. Grünewald's Crucifixions are like no other Crucifixions. Christ is blood-spattered, abject, ugly, and festered with abscesses as were the bodies with St. Anthony's fire in the hospital of the monastery for whose chapel the great Isenheim altarpiece was painted. His Christs are human, but they are fearsome and awe-inspiring. In Grünewald is the germ of today's expressionism. He paints against a medieval background with all the details of traditional religious art, but his intense emotion is personal and individualistic. Thus, like Michelangelo, Tintoretto, and El Greco, he is one of the really great Christian religious painters.

Art has long recognized a change that came over the Renaissance and was seen early in the work of Michelangelo and Tintoretto and was later revealed in the paintings of Pontormo, Rosso, Parmigianino, and Bronzino. This change was a break between the Renaissance and the Baroque; and because it is so closely related to art today it has taken on new importance, and the artists once laughed at are now taken seriously. With their broken and elongated forms and colors they sought to extinguish all physical and sensual things. Their compositions were based on spirals and zigzags. This intensely expressive style spread throughout Europe, and is now known as Mannerism. The striving for spiritual depth and inwardness of Mannerism had an intellectual affinity with the painting of Michelangelo. Tintoretto was also basically a Mannerist. He followed in the footsteps of Michelangelo, and at the same time his work has the germ of the Baroque seventeenth century.

The mystic manner and imaginative conceptions of Tintoretto are reflected in the work of El Greco, who also had an intense, passionate style, and made dramatic use of light and flame-like rhythmic forms. Indeed, it is difficult to draw the line between centuries of art, for although an artist may belong in one century because of his dates, the characteristics and spirit of his work may place him in the age before or the age after. El Greco is an example. His forms tend toward the Baroque, but his spirit is mystic and medieval. Although the spirit of the forms alternates with the tides of history, an artist often intuitively shifts his techniques before social changes become apparent.

CHAPTER VIII
ROMAN CATHOLIC BAROQUE ART

To express ecstasy art made use of all its incantations, all its magic of light and shadow.

—Emile Mâle

It is difficult to define a period that includes so many different forms and spheres of culture as we see in the contemporaries of the seventeenth century—Caravaggio, the Carracci and Bernini in Italy, Poussin in France, El Greco and Velásquez in Spain, the Asams and Balthasar Neumann in the Germanic countries, Christopher Wren in England, and Rubens, Rembrandt, and van Dyck in the Netherlands. However, in all its forms, whether architecture, painting, sculpture, or goldsmiths' work, Baroque asserts itself in spectacular splendor and in overstatement. Mass, space, height, color, and light combine in robust grandeur. Baroque accepts the Classic tradition and form of the Renaissance, but breaks the structure into movement. Great columns and masses in motion break out of the picture frame and extend into space and infinity—diagonals, foreshortenings, exaggerated effects of light and shade, and oversized foregrounds give a dramatic effect and draw us into the picture. Architecture, sculpture, and painting all bulge in plastic modeled form. Sculpture is moving and doing rather than contemplating. The cartouche is a basic Baroque motif; "C" and "S" curves and volutes, twisted columns, broken pediments, voluminous draperies and exaggerated gestures are characteristic elements of this materialistic, fleshy style. The naturalism of Caravaggio and the emotionalism of the Carracci represent the two directions that the style took.

Although the Carracci are not accorded great importance in the history of art, we must give them our attention here because of their connection with the Church and the painting of the Counter Reformation. Their painting transformed the involved symbolism of Christian art into a formula of clear symbols such as the halo, the lily, the cross, and the crescent. They initiated the scenes of ecstasies, of adoration and suffering and the pious look with upturned eyes that later became characteristic of the sickly sweet paintings of Carlo Dolci and finally the language of the hackneyed art of the Church Supply. The Carracci also resolved such subjects as the Annunciation, Birth of Christ, Baptism, Christ Carrying the Cross, the Good Samaritan, the Penitent Magdalen, Christ as the Gardener, and the Crown of Thorns into the forms that became the models for today's devotional image. Yet the Carraccis themselves were good, if not great, painters. They emphasize the material element of Christian art, and their paintings are earthbound and understandable. Lodovico Carracci's "The Immaculate Conception" introduces a prototype for a new pattern that becomes popular later, in the paintings of Murillo. The Madonna floats on the crescent moon against a light-colored nimbus and clouds. The Carracci school trained a host of artists, including Domenichino, Guido Reni, Lanfranco, Albani, Guercino, Carlo Dolci, and Pozzo, who decorated churches and painted religious subjects throughout the seventeenth century.

Caravaggio, although rejected for his coarse realism, had a great influence on artists of both Italy and Spain, and today he is recognized as an initiator of modern art. Although Caravaggio was a Classicist, he broke with the past and presented his subjects with originality, vigor, and intense energy. He attains plastic vigor of mass by the dramatic use of light and employs dark and light to express violent emotion. Caravaggio's pictures were often criticized by the Church because they did not edify and because he did not show the nobility and sublimity considered essential for a religious picture. Yet his pictures and altarpieces present a powerful religious drama told in a new way and with new visual symbols. He treated the supernatural as reality, humanized the saints, and brought the miraculous down to earth. His idea of the perception of the spiritual by means of the senses was not new. It is implied in the aesthetics of Thomas Aquinas, in Thomas a Kempis' *De Imitatione Christi,* and in the *Spiritual Exercises* of Loyola, which set the basic religious mood of the Baroque. Caravaggio's religious scenes are expressed in terms of the common people. His characters are peasants instead of kings and queens, and the emphasis is on the corporal and realistic, but the artistic use of light tells the story. In "The Calling of Matthew" the light centers on the hand and face of Christ. In "The Supper at Emmaus" in the Brera, Milan, a spiritual light engulfs the form of Christ and leaves the unessentials in shadow. This forced dramatic use of light influenced the work of Rubens and Ribera and even led to the luminous style of Rembrandt.

Although the Church used Baroque art and architecture to further its own ends and purposes, the Church did not create the Baroque style; it did, however, influence the content. The subject matter of Baroque art is religious, and in Italy, Spain, and Germany it is Roman Catholic. The most important works of architects, sculptors, and painters were commissioned by the Church or given to the Church by wealthy patrons. The Church realized anew that the aesthetic approach could open the way for a deeper religious meaning, and it sought the aid of art to make the service more pleasing. The church building was turned into an attractive, resplendent place that appealed to the senses and at the same time pointed to ascetic severity of religious expression.

Artists were required to conform to canonical form of Biblical stories and the official interpretation of dogma for the purposes of propaganda. In order to do this, the Church adopted a twofold program: first, to reaffirm certain dogmas; second, to encourage the use of Her sacraments and observance of rituals such as the veneration of images. This required the faithful to take the point of view defined by the Church, which in the main sought to reaffirm all those dogmas that were criticized by Luther and other reformers. The supremacy of the papacy was reasserted, and the formulation of this doctrine was seen in the dramatic Throne of St. Peter by Bernini in St. Peter's, Rome. The Virgin was exalted and her purity established by the dogma of the Immaculate Conception. The sacrament of Penance brought the figures of St. Peter and Mary Magdalen to the fore in the iconography of Counter Reformation art, and the sacrament of the Eucharist is represented in such subjects as the Last Communion of St. Jerome. Works of charity were defended, and Catholic saints and martyrs such as St. Theresa and St. Charles Borromeo were venerated for their miraculous visions and ecstasy. Thus the scenes of the Gospel took on a new iconography, and Heaven came down to earth in such subjects as the Annunciation and the Nativity. The scenes of the Passion also take on a new importance, and new devotional exercises include the Holy Family, the Child Jesus, St. Joseph, the Sacred Heart, and the Guardian Angels. The subject of the Death's Head or "Vanite" appears, and scenes of death and agony are compared to the sufferings of Christ. Such symbols as the pelican, a symbol of Christ on the Cross; the phoenix, symbol of the Resurrection of Christ; the unicorn, symbol of Christ and chastity; the serpent, symbol of Christ crucified; the IHS within rays, and the eye of God came into use at this time. This was the iconography of Christian Humanism as taught by the Jesuits, and it formed a new conception of the Bible that was intelligible and accepted by the masses. The Counter Reformation did not condemn Renaissance Humanism; it merely sought to put decency back into Christian art and to preserve the *status quo* of the Church. By the decrees of the Council of Trent the artists of this period were under the strict control of the Church. All art required the approval of the bishop. Subjects emphasized the theological or the supernatural in religion but the artists were obliged to keep closely to the Biblical story, which must be made clear and accurate without picturesque or local detail. No image or painting could suggest false doctrine. Angels must have wings and saints halos and proper attributes, and no nudes were allowed. In martyrdoms and the sufferings of Christ the painter was obliged to show the grimness and horror of the scene, while a calmer beauty was prescribed for such subjects as the Baptism or Transfiguration. The rules were strict, but within these bounds the artist could use color, clouds, and draperies that produced a worldly, emotional type of art that stirred the emotions and senses of the people and thus related the religious art to life. But the Counter Reformation Church placed greatest emphasis on the two dogmas of Benevolent Charity and the Blessed Sacrament. Subjects of art show acts of mercy such as Elizabeth tending the sick and St. Martin sharing his cloak with the beggar. The Last Supper, which in the past had most frequently depicted the moment of Judas' betrayal, now chose the moment of the consecration of the Host. Instead of simple miracles such as the raising of Lazarus, artists portrayed moments of ecstasy and mysticism in the lives of the saints. The Baroque artist was devout, and eagerly agreed to use his skill in proclaiming the dogmas of the Catholic Faith. The bellwether of the Baroque, Michelangelo, became obsessed with the salvation of his soul. Tiepolo belonged to the Confraternity of Mount Carmel; Carlo Dolci would paint only devotional subjects; and Pacheco, the erudite Spanish painter, teacher, and author, wrote in his book *The Art of Painting:* "The aim of painting is the service of God."

Although the Counter Reformation was the main driving force in the development of Baroque Roman Catholic Church art and architecture, the Church did not get its program under way for some years after the Council of Trent (1545–1563).

Carlo Moderna was the architect of the nave and façade of St. Peter's in 1626. But the most significant work in Baroque was accomplished some years later by the architects Borromini, Pietro da Cortona, and Bernini. The great Gesù Church had been planned by Michelangelo, who also heralded the Baroque in the massive dome of St. Peter's. However, the Gesù was built by Giacamo da Vignola after the death of Michelangelo, and is Mannerist in its broken and unbalanced proportions, although it contains Baroque characteristics and is the forerunner of later Baroque churches. The ground plan combines the central plan of the Renaissance with the longitudinal basilica plan. The Jesuits dispensed with choral offices, and shared the services with the congregation. Thus they eliminated the screen. A shallow apse provided a view of the altar. The light is handled in a new way, and becomes a positive factor in the architectural design. Windows of plain glass, concealed behind pillars in side chapels, high in the dome, or on the west wall behind the worshipers, are arranged so that the light falls on certain areas of the architecture and decoration. The nave is lighted by windows above the side chapels that give a subdued light, darker in the last bay before the dome; and from the dome and cupola a flood of light streams down in a startling glow before the altar. Small windows in the apse give light on the altar, thus focusing attention on the altar. Jesuit churches up to this time were somber and austere; and the Gesù, which was the epitome, also had little embellishment when it was first built. It was Vignola's plan that was different. "The Triumph of the Name of Jesus," by Giovanni Gaulli, which forms the fresco decoration of the Gesù, was not added until later.

In the characteristic Baroque church both the architectural masses and the decoration are full of energy and rhythmical momentum. Early Baroque concentrates in one powerful rhythm; High Baroque art expands and bursts into many movements and broken masses of forms. The walls are molded, and surfaces swing in convex or concave forms. The High Baroque becomes a structure of oval and circle that binds in a sense of community worship, yet points to the altar. There are no columns or arcades to impede the view or transepts to interfere with the central space. Though the architectural features—pilasters, entablatures, arches, and vaults—are the same as those of the Renaissance, they are combined and used differently. Perspective, color, and grouping are a union of the visible and invisible, and earth and Heaven are brought together in a pageantry of color, symbol worship, and communion. Numbers are used with both aesthetic and symbolic meanings: three represents the Trinity; five, the Wounds of Christ; seven, the Words from the Cross or the Sorrows of Mary; twelve, the Apostles. Steps are planned symbolically in groups of threes or sevens, and pillars or windows are grouped in threes or twelves. The wealth of decorative detail—paintings, stucco, and statuary—is massed in profusion. Multitudes of angels, cherubs, sacred signs, and rays of light crowd about the holy figures in joyous curves and volutes, but all has order and an inner unity. Side altars by means of slant and asymmetrical design lead the eye to the main altar. Statues are grouped in attitudes that are traditional, and great visionary frescoes have one theme. There is an echo of Gothic aspiration in the dome frescoes that reach into infinite perspective, but the Baroque church included the earthly order and accepted the world and used it as a symbol and reflection of the heavenly world. By means of figures, color, grouping, and symbol, art uses angels, saints, Prophets, and martyrs with a message that connects the earthly with the heavenly; and by this method Baroque recaptured the religious spirit of the past.

The themes of Baroque dome frescoes included: the redemption of man through the mercy of God in sending His Son; the glorification of the Holy Trinity; the life of Christ or Mary, culminating in the Resurrection, Ascension, Assumption, or Coronation; Mary as intercessor; the life of a patron saint and his glorification; the story of a pilgrimage treated historically, theologically, or as legend. The frescoes were arranged on the walls of the sanctuary and above the high altar and in the dome, and were so arranged that the themes connected the altar and the dome in an upward movement.

Color was intensified as it went upward or toward the altar, and red was usually used about the altar. Figures in a Baroque altarpiece always look upward, pointing our attention to the scene above—the Madonna soars, the Magdalene glances upward.

Subsidiary themes were above the side altars and the organ at the main entrance. The painting in the dome gave an effect of sky, but with a religious pageant taking place that shows the shining splendor of the Church. The glowing colors and atmospheric effect produced a mystical splendor the effect of which was overwhelming. The architectural setting was an ideal background for this Baroque art and for the joyful, triumphant religion therein enacted. Dome painters of early Italian Baroque include Guido Reni, who in his small paintings carried on the work of the Carracci and idealized the figures of Christ, the Madonnas, Mater Dolorosas, and Magdalenes with a sublime, sensuous grace that the people relished. Domenichino, Albani, and Lanfranco also decorated churches in the early Baroque period.

The most influential artist of the High Baroque was Giovanni Bernini, who was both architect and sculptor, and whose best known works are the St. Teresa in the Cornaro Chapel of Santa Maria della Vittoria, Rome, and the Cathedra and Baldacchino in St. Peter's. The Cathedra is a spiritual symbol that must be judged in the light of the Catholic Faith rather than from the standpoint of art. It is composed of rich marbles and bronze gilt and floats on clouds surrounded by angels and the dove of the Holy Spirit depicted in translucent glass. The St. Teresa is remarkable for its intense visual language of expression and gesture and for the dramatic settings created for the individual sculptures. The St. Teresa is placed within a niche. Beams of gold metal shafts conceal the back wall of the niche; from an opening above, a magical yellow light is shed over the scene, and a closely calculated integration unites the sculptured group with the intent of the church. This is the most ecstatic Baroque sculpture in Italy, and is to be matched only by the "Trasparente" in Toledo Cathedral, Spain. Bernini also completed the colonnades of St. Peter's and designed several distinctive small churches in the form of Greek crosses, circles, or ovals with a dome.

Pietro da Cortona, the architect of the church of Santa Maria della Pace, Rome, was also a painter. He planned and painted some of the most impressive domes of the Italian High Baroque. Andrea Pozzo's famous ceiling in San Ignazio, "The Glorification of the Company of Jesus," is the culmination of the effect of light and infinitude in Baroque domes. The High Baroque was reached under the influence of the architect Borromini. Borromini broke with traditional styles and looked to nature for his original architectural detail and daring rhythms. The Church of San Ivo alla Sapienza and the Spada Chapel represent his work at its best.

In France, the best-known French artist of the seventeenth century who painted Biblical subjects was Nicolas Poussin. He held himself aloof from such Baroque artists as Bernini, and was influenced by Classic antiquity and the painting of Raphael. He painted many pictures illustrating both the Old and New Testaments and also did two series of paintings of the Seven Sacraments, but he seldom accepted Church commissions. His paintings have the composition structure of the Renaissance, as well as a classical coldness, yet at the same time they reveal a lyrical warmth, especially in the use of landscape. The importance of Poussin's religious pictures lies in the dramatic action and the gist of the moral epigram. He sought to depict historically correct costumes, manners, and scenery. Scenes in Egypt have pyramids and palm trees as settings. In the Eucharist, or Last Supper, in the Louvre, the Apostles are lying on couches around the table. The painting chooses a moment both sacramental and dramatic. Christ has given the bread and is about to bless the cup; Judas is just leaving the room. Poussin's paintings have a disciplined Baroque feeling. Rhythm and proportion are as carefully balanced as in architecture, and the emotions are controlled, but his use of landscape to echo the figure composition has a poetry that breathes of eternity, stillness, and abstract grandeur. Painting at the same time as Poussin was a provincial artist, Georges de La Tour. His paintings have the mystic emotion of simple faith, and tell a quiet story with deep devotion. His candle-lit pictures might be called Christian nocturnes.

The revival of church decoration and altarpiece painting in France did not come until late in the seventeenth century, under the influence of Colbert and the artist Charles Le Brun, who followed the style of the Italian dome painters. The Church of the Invalides, designed by Mansart, and the Church of the Assumption were decorated with huge frescoes by Charles de la Fosse. Antoine Coypel painted the frescoes in the Chapel at Versailles, and Jean Jouvenet also painted religious subjects. But art becomes centered on the king, Louis XIV, and both historical and religious subjects are used for his glorification in the decoration of palaces instead of churches.

The spirit of the Counter Reformation and Baroque art spread from Italy into southern Germany and Austria. In Bavaria early Jesuit Baroque churches were built by Italian architects and later by architects and artists of Germany influenced by Italian designs of Bernini and Borromini and the frescoes of Tiepolo in the Residenz at Würzburg. The most important creators of the German Baroque were the Asam brothers and Balthasar Neumann. The Asams were architects, painters, and sculptors, and they combined their arts in the building and decoration of churches. By means of atmosphere and vision, they created a great religious pageant of mystical import in the churches of Weltenburg and St. John Nepomuk in Munich; and in many other churches built by various architects they were the decorators. In the Church of St. John Nepomuk the dome fresco has the theme of "The Coronation of the Virgin," and the symbolic group of statuary above the high altar is that of the Holy Trinity. All elements seem to combine with the architecture into a complete whole expressing the epitome of Baroque religious fervor and joyousness. The great tableau of the Resurrection of the Virgin in the abbey church at Rohr is set as a dramatic focal point above the high altar. Life-size apostles stand above the Baroque sarcophagus, and the Virgin rises to Heaven supported by angels with clouds and cherubs in a startling, melodramatic scene. These are typical of the many Baroque churches with painted domes and dramatic altar showpieces, gilded rays, and exaggerated lighting effects.

The fantastic quality of German Baroque art is matched only by that of Spain. Baroque reached a late development in Spain, but the art of the Counter Reformation found an ideal setting in monkish Roman Catholic Spain and in the work of El Greco. El Greco was influenced by the work of Michelangelo as well as by that of Tintoretto and Titian, but his spirit is that of Catholic Spain. We enjoy the work of El Greco for its richness, variety, and rhythmic vitality that is achieved by means of the structural pattern of dark and light values. The flamelike vertical swirls and streakings give an intensified visual effectiveness. In "The Agony in the Garden," in the National Gallery in London, El Greco conceives the scene with more interest in its symbolical meaning than in the physical representation of the scene. By deliberately distorting the forms and lighting, he achieves drama and spiritual meaning. The structural design of the figures is woven into the setting. Behind the figure of Christ is a rock that echoes the form of His Figure, and the cloud behind the angel repeats the shape of the angel's wings; the sleeping disciples are enveloped within a cavelike form, and the whole scene consists of meandering diagonals of light. Thus the setting has produced a mood that intensifies the meaning and stresses the contrast between the ethereal and earthy that makes this picture the most Christian of all such scenes since the early representations on carved ivory.

El Greco's use of distortion, clouds, drapery, and dramatic lighting is seen in his various Crucifixions. The elongated body of Christ in strong white light is hung upon the Cross amid a setting of moving dark cloud masses of turbulent grandeur that express the emotional impact and depth of feeling of the scene. El Greco's concern was with the troubled states of the soul. The bodies of his figures are gaunt and unearthly, and the sickly greens, cool blues, lemon-yellows, and wine-reds which are usually kept secondary to the browns and grays give his paintings a sepulchral character. It is the expression of the conflict of the Spanish Inquisition dealt with in an intense medieval manner. Though El Greco was a devout Catholic, he was not in favor with the Church, and he painted to express his own deep religious feelings of ecstasy and penitence rather than to please any patron. In his day he was seldom recognized, and his ascetic painting had few followers. Instead, Spanish painters were fascinated by the naturalism of Caravaggio, and this is shown both in the choice of subject matter and in the intense realism of the paintings of Francisco de Ribalta and of José Ribera.

Ribera painted tortures and martyrdoms, and beggars and wrinkled old men were his favorite models. Francisco de Zurbarán was also influenced by Caravaggio, and is known for his paintings of ecstatic monks. His paintings have deep religious fervor and are typical of the religious asceticism of Spain of the seventeenth century. Other painters and interpreters of the Jesuit tradition of Spain include the sculptor Alonso Berruguete, whose figures combine pathos and torment; Luis de Morales, Juan de las Roelas, Luis de Vargas, Francisco Pacheco, and Francisco de Herrera, the Elder. Pacheco established a workshop in Seville and sent works of religious art to decorate churches in Mexico and South America. His paintings of the Immaculate Conception are unique in that they usually depict the Virgin standing on a crescent in which is a scene of the harbor and landscape of Seville.

Velásquez was trained in the workshop of Pacheco, and his early religious paintings show Pacheco's influence, although the details of his iconography are original. Although Velásquez painted "The Adoration of the Magi," "The Coronation of the Virgin," "Christ and the Christian Soul," "Christ and the Pilgrims at Emmaus," "The Immaculate Conception" and other, lesser-known religious subjects, his pictures lack deep spirituality.

The most popular painter of the Spanish seventeenth century was Bartolomé Murillo, the painter of the Virgin. His Virgin was human and theatrical, but she spoke to the people of the joys of Heaven in a language that moved and touched. Murillo's paintings have a sense of infinity. His flesh tones reflect light, and he makes light and air tell of ethereal experiences by means of his power of conception, composition, and workmanship, although his work is sweet and somewhat suave. Juan de Valdés Leal painted "The Immaculate Conception" in the visionary tradition of El Greco.

The realistic sculptor of seventeenth century Spain was Juan Martínez Montañes, who produced the terrifying mournful and intense subjects the Spanish love so well. His crucifixes are true to life and realistic but at the same time sublime. Also typically Spanish are the figures of the Passion made for use during Lent by Gregorio Hernández. These realistic figures of Christ suffering in chains, bleeding under the crown of thorns, and struggling beneath the weight of the Cross are unique in Spanish and Latin American art of the seventeenth and eighteenth centuries.

The ivory crucifix, one of the important articles of Roman Catholic devotion, became popular at this time. It was made by ivory sculptors in France, Germany, and the Netherlands in the seventeenth century. A few such crucifixes had been made in the Middle Ages, but now they were in demand for altars, screens, and private devotions. The typical seventeenth century ivory crucifix depicts Christ in a realistic position, the face showing suffering. The ivory figure is nailed to a cross of ebony wood with three or four nails and usually has a crown of thorns. These figures were often colored and jeweled. Although some of these crucifixes are by known sculptors, they are all of one type and seldom show any originality. Ivory crucifixes continued to be made in great numbers from that time down to the present.

There were two important Flemish Christian painters of the seventeenth century. The most famous was Peter Paul Rubens, who painted altarpieces and church decorations for the Jesuits. His masterpieces "The Elevation of the Cross" and "The Descent from the Cross" were painted for the Antwerp Cathedral. In these paintings his dynamic spiraling forms and his fluid color give a universal vision of life, but he has little mysticism or deep spiritual communication. His large painting of the Last Judgment is a human avalanche of forms with expressions of horror and anguish increased by dramatic effects of light and flames. He paints with warm glowing yellows, vermilions, and pearly blues, and achieves a brilliant realism combined with idealism. His Madonnas have a plump, sensuous quality.

Anton van Dyck was a pupil of Rubens, but he did not have the force and vigor of his teacher. Although a Baroque painter, he seems essentially Protestant in his choice of subject matter. His "Tribute Money" is one of his best-known paintings. The face of Christ is the center of the composition, with the head given prominence by the light background of the sky, and there is contrast in tone, expression, and character between Christ and the figures of the two questioning men. Van Dyck also painted several Crucifixions, the Holy Family, Apostles, "Lamentation over Christ," and "The Descent of the Holy Ghost," which employs a dramatic use of light. He paints with religious feeling and more sentiment and tenderness of feeling than Rubens. He seems to feel the agony and sadness of the Crucifixion scene, interpreting the tragedy through the eyes of love, and he gives purity and mother love to the Virgin; but although he expressed piety and godliness, his sense of religion and artistic conception are not profound.

Baroque art is not the greatest Christian art the world has known. It is fleshy, sensory, and theatrical. It lacks composure and restraint; it is overdecorative; and it has puffy marshmallow forms and colors. However, the materialism of Baroque was sanctioned by the Church, notably in its permission to use images and in the dogma of Transubstantiation. Withal it was the perfect interpreter of Loyola, St. Theresa, seventeenth century ecstasies and martyrdoms, and of a Faith that found little repose in an age of Protestant attacks without and a militant Church within. Baroque at its best depicted a sincere regeneration of the Christian Faith, and as long as this spiritual ardor lasted, art was vital and sincere; but it finally declined into cheap pomposity. Although it was gorgeous and sensuous and had technical excellence, in the hands of lesser artists it became mechanical, lost its great conception, and for the most part became a glorification of the Jesuit Order more than a devout expression of the Faith.

"In order to understand the poetry of the Baroque one must have seen Mass being celebrated at St. Peter's or any Jesuit church in Europe. Thanks to the grace of the liturgy, in the perfumed mist of incense and organ music one sees no longer a mere world of marble and paint, a human world, but a great composition in which the movement of the painted figures and the ritual of the priests combine in a grand symphony. . . . The Catholic Church, which from time immemorial has known how to stimulate fervor in the faithful by appealing to the senses, offered the Christian of the Counter Reformation an accessible image of the beyond—an operatic spectacle." Thus wrote Germain Bazin in *A History of Art.* But with all the pomp and circumstance, there is an absence of the awe-inspiring mystical quality in Baroque art. It lacks the silence and space that we find in Romanesque and Cistercian churches, qualities that compel awe and worship and adoration in the deepest sense.

CHAPTER IX

ART OF THE PROTESTANT REFORMATION

In the sixteenth century when Luther protested against indulgences and other corruptions of the Roman Catholic Church, he lit the spark of the Reformation that gave birth to Protestantism, and Protestantism brought about changes in both the art and architecture of the church. The resulting changes of the Reformation were different in the Roman Catholic than in the Protestant Church. The Roman Catholic Church took the defensive and sought to proclaim and defend all the dogma and doctrines rejected and criticized by the Protestants. For her defense, the Roman Catholic Church chose the radical Baroque style. In this decision the Church was wise, for Baroque was "up to date" and its appearance was pompous and impressive. It was not necessary for the Roman Catholic Church to make architectural changes, for church architecture through the ages had been developed for the cult of Catholicism and the needs of its liturgy and service, and the continuity of the Roman Catholic Church saved the ancient architecture. But it was necessary for the Protestants to develop a new style of architecture to fit the needs of their changed liturgy and the participation of the congregation in the service. The many divisions of the Protestant Church called for various individual changes. It took some years for the Protestant churches to define their needs clearly; in the meantime the old Roman Catholic church buildings were made to serve. When adaptations were made they were often crudely utilitarian.

It was natural for the Protestants to reject glorifying Baroque art, but on the whole the Protestant Church repudiated art instead of redefining the place of art in religion. For the main part they forsook art as a vanity and dispensed with the warmth and color that art could provide. For fear of losing God in the enjoyment of God's creation, they suppressed the sensual and mystical values of religion in favor of the moral values. The church was purged of images, paintings of idolatry, and the ritual of the Mass, and thus in the Protestant Church art no longer had a recognized participation in divine worship. No longer was the church a vast sacramental work of art that drew all the arts into its service. When the church ceased to be a composite work of art, religious art withdrew to the homes of the people, and there, for a short time, private devotional paintings continued the vital Christian spirit.

The Church in the past had often been negligent or antagonistic toward art. It had used it freely or feared it. Though the intensity of the Jews' realization of God's greatness made them fear the image, iconoclasticism produced some of the world's finest decorative art and the literature of the Hebrew Prophets. In the twelfth century the Cistercians condemned stained glass and images; but their puritanism, by means of form and fine proportion, produced some of the greatest church architecture of all time. Savonarola condemned the use of nudes and contemporary portraits in religious painting, but through his influence Botticelli, Michelangelo, and other Renaissance artists painted some of their greatest pictures. The puritanism of the Reformation produced great religious music, but Rembrandt is the only really significant painter who felt the influence of the Reformation.

However, the leaders of the Reformation were not so unfriendly toward the visual arts as is generally thought. Even Calvin writes: "Yet am I not so scrupulous as to judge that no images should be endured or suffered; but seeing that the art of painting and carving images cometh from God, I require that the practise of art should be kept pure and lawful. . . . Therefore men should not paint or carve anything but such as can be seen with the eye; so that God's Majesty, which is too exalted for human sight, may not be corrupted by fantasies which have no true agreement therewith." Luther went further: "The Law of Moses forbade only the image of God; the crucifix is not forbidden." He would have church walls painted with the Creation, and Noah building the Ark, and wished he could persuade lords and gentlemen to have the whole of the Bible painted outside and inside their homes. When Karlstadt broke images and glass at Wittenberg, Luther protested. In addition, Luther was the friend of Dürer and Lucas Cranach, and Lutheran churches were decorated with painted reredos and carved crucifixes.* One of the finest examples of Lutheran art was the reredos painted by Hans Leonard Schäufelein which included parables relating to Protestantism. Though Zwingli removed and destroyed images, even he protected stained glass, "since it led to no risk of idolatry."

The emphasis of the Protestant leaders was on reason and intellect, and they refused to admit the advantages of external aids to devotion or beauty of the edifice to attract people to church. Yet for many years Protestantism did nothing to check the lavish decoration of churches, and continued to use the churches built by Catholicism; even the great tabernacles were permitted to remain in Lutheran churches, although they were no longer used for their original purpose.

It was the difference in outlook between the Roman Catholic Church and the Protestant churches of the Reformation that brought about the different approach to the arts. Although Protestantism was not art-minded, neither was the Roman Catholic Church interested in the aesthetic value of art. The images for them were not works of art but symbols and objects of veneration.

Early Christian art was based on the Old Testament, which describes art objects, and the early Church was guided by descriptions of form, color, and symbolism in the building of places of worship. All the arts were called to the service of the Church for the making of holy vessels and garments for the priest, and this tradition lasted down through the ages until the Reformation, which put the emphasis on the spirit of the Gospels of the New Testament, writings that were not concerned with art. In the New Testament there are no rules or descriptions of how the church should be built or how the altar should be vested, for the New Testament was the revelation of a person, not a code of rules.

Our Lord and His Disciples are silent on the subject of objects of art. Yet the beauty and imagery of nature is everywhere present in the sermons and parables of our Lord, and in His teachings He used the visible: the bread and wine, the cup, the bowl of water, the towel, the alabaster box—all products of the craftsmanship of glass, of stone, of wood, of the loom—the externals of worship to emphasize the spiritual and the eternal.

Luther too was devoted to imagery. His writings are full of it, and it gave him joy to picture events. Through Luther's translation of the Bible the beautiful imagery of many Bible passages was given to the modern world. Luther and Protestantism were not interested in the pomp and glitter of the medieval church of Rome, which were further intensified by the Baroque style, but in the simple, the natural, and the genuine. Luther wished the Virgin portrayed to show "how the exceeding riches of God joined in her with her utter poverty, the divine honor with her low estate, the divine glory with her shame, the divine greatness with her smallness, the divine goodness with her lack of merit, the divine grace with her unworthiness." Thus it appeared to him that the duty of religious art was to show how the divine and sublime appeared in the lowly and contemptible. Rembrandt expressed what Luther desired. Later Eduard von Gebhardt and Fritz von Uhde also expressed the fundamental Protestant religious feeling in art that delighted in paradox—a spiritual content in the lowly, a religion at home in a small room.

While the art of the Counter Reformation represented Christ in the resplendence of His divine nature, the Protestants sought to depict Christ as a servant, a Son of God become Man. In the words of W. A. Visser't Hooft, "Rubens' pictures of Christ may fill us with awe, those of Guido Reni with compassion, but they never confront us with another world," and they do not tell us of the great mystery of the Christ. Christian art of this kind does not leave room for faith. Yet Rembrandt, who expressed the beliefs of the Reformation and the quiet voice of the Bible, was rejected, and instead the Protestant Church embraced the art expressing the doctrines, dogma, and pomp of the Roman Catholic Church. Furthermore, because the average man of the seventeenth century prized realism and the skill of visual representation, he was unable to appreciate an artist who transcended that approach, and geniuses like Rembrandt were ignored in favor of the unimaginative artist with flawless workmanship.

The Reformation forced the Christian artist to stand face to face with the Gospel and interpret it as he felt it, rather than by the dictates of tradition. Thus the seventeenth century restated Christian art and found new solutions. The Protestant Reformation changed the whole religious scene of art. It was natural that the subject matter of Protestant art of the Reformation should differ from Roman Catholic art of the same era. The devotional picture that was a simple and sincere expression of faith disappeared, for it belonged to the Roman Catholic Church. Saints and altarpieces with themes of saints were no longer in demand. The scenes of Inferno and the Doom or Last Judgment disappeared. The miraculous was put in the background together with emotional and lyrical elements; Biblical subjects were approached from the human side; and the human and divine were fused. The awareness of the divine element in human nature and the Incarnation of the Savior-God made man are the dominant themes of the art of the Protestant Reformation, which in a way foreshadowed nineteenth century humanitarianism. Christ's miracles were made visible in such subjects as the Supper at Emmaus and the Raising of Lazarus. The parables were also favorite subjects, especially the parable of the Prodigal Son. Christ became the healer and friend. Protestant art taught the value of the common task and daily work, and art was brought into the homes of the low and simple by means of inexpensive prints. The identification of religion with the individual is a special mark of Protestant art.

Although Rembrandt was the greatest Protestant painter, his religious paintings are unecclesiastic. They are neither Roman Catholic nor Protestant nor Jewish, nor do they contain dogma or symbols of the divine order; instead, they probe the depths of the mystery of life. To Rembrandt the life of Christ was the life of every man. He treats the Person and acts of Christ without mysticism. But he makes the divine aspect convincing in the homely aspect. He expresses the human joys and sorrows, the sympathy, friendliness, and warmth of feeling of family life. His portrayal of Christ's acts of ministry are epic, and eternal love is expressed in the parable of the Prodigal Son.

With Rembrandt the concept of the subject was of first importance; the form came afterward and was governed by the content. He was a profound interpreter of the human soul and his keen interest in human characterization was based on a personal and universal vision. He chose for his illustrations the stories of the Bible that best illuminate the human situation and show the majesty of God. The famous "Hundred Guilder Print" shows Christ healing the sick and welcoming children. "The Supper at Emmaus" reveals the mysterious radiance of the celestial world. In his Holy Family and Adoration of the Shepherds there is a fusion of human and divine, of Biblical and genre. His handling of light and light and shadow without detail crosses the boundaries of the visible and suggests the impending beyond. The legendary antiquity of the Biblical drama is reflected in Rembrandt's fantastic rabbis and voluptuous Jewesses. His palette is made up of monochrome russets and reds with compelling streaks of dramatic light. His materials are somber deep-textured fabrics, velvet, and furs, and jewels from the depths of the mine, but they too radiate light.

Rembrandt received no commissions from the Church, but he chose to paint Biblical scenes because of his study and love of the Bible. In his early life he painted heroic scenes from the Old Testament in the dramatic theatrical language of the Baroque style. Later, Rembrandt's painting shows an inner change and takes on a deeper dimension. He becomes concerned with the content and meaning of the Bible, and his painting reflects the simplicity, stillness, and quietness of Biblical prose, and seeks to interpret it or rather to let it speak for itself. He becomes particularly interested in the story of Abraham, of the Good Samaritan, of Christ at Emmaus, themes of the individual human being meeting God, or of the teaching and healing Christ; of the humanity of the Virgin and the temptation and tribulation of Christ. The Christ of Rembrandt is a human Christ. Rembrandt paints the Christ who heals, the Christ who forgives, the Christ who bears the sins of the world, and the risen Christ made perfect through suffering. Rembrandt's Virgin is a humble woman who "ponders all things in her heart." She is the Mary of Calvin and of Luther who wrote, "The more we attribute deserving merit to her, the more we take away from divine grace and lessen the truth of the Magnificat." The beauty, greatness, and poetry of the traditional Madonna are taken away to stress her lowliness and to emphasize the infinite distance between God and Man.

For many years Protestantism had no architecture suited to its needs. According to Karl Holl, in *The Cultural Significance of the Reformation,* the fact that in the worship service Luther had not really created anything new, but had been content with a purification of tradition, prevented Protestantism from reaching clarity over the purpose of the church building. The existing churches with their altars, crucifix, and carved or painted reredos were used, and although images were removed there was no occasion to build new churches. In Germany architects began to experiment with new ideas for church architecture before the Church itself defined its purpose. Although the altar was retained, the sacrament and ministry were given different emphasis, and preaching and doctrinal teaching gave the pulpit greater importance. As early as 1570 the pulpit was put in the nave and the organ over the altar. The Lutherans in Germany accepted the Baroque style of architecture, and churches were built in circular, square, and triangular shapes with balconies. By 1600 the altar, pulpit, and organ were placed one above another and combined in one carved Baroque structure. The importance of music in the German church of the Reformation made many of the churches look like an opera house. In the Frauenkirche in Dresden there are balconies and boxes, and the chancel is set as a stage and steps lead to the altar, which has exposed organ pipes above and behind it.

Rectangular churches were also built with font, altar, pulpit, and organ grouped together so that the congregation could both see and hear. The altar with crucifix and candles was in a niche under and in front of the pulpit. In the new churches the walls were whitewashed, and representations of Luther, Melanchthon, and the Apostles were painted on the walls. These churches had flat ceilings and family pews and an air of domesticity. With church music and preaching given such importance and the sacrament and liturgy minimized, the central church seemed to fill the practical needs of congregational worship. Although it was wanting in color and mystical values, the German church of the Reformation was spacious, restful, and dignified.

The Dutch church of the seventeenth century retained the traditional cruciform plan with a high roof and steeple. The interior was simple Gothic with a chancel but no altar. There was little decoration, but the organ cases and the covered preaching pulpit with winding staircase were carved and decorated and a few pictures were hung on the otherwise bare interiors with their white walls and clear glass. The interiors were as simple and dignified as the faith. There are paintings of these interiors by the well-known church painters of the school of Delft. In the paintings of Utrecht churches by Pieter Saenredam there is a calm and beautiful simplicity created by fine proportion and space. Tall windows with clear glass and huge brass chandeliers are the setting for the high pulpits with sounding boards and winding staircases and the large exposed organ pipes decorated with simple Gothic tracery. These church interiors are extended still-life paintings with quiet presence and actionless existence. The Calvinistic churches of Switzerland were also austere. There was no altar, and the communion table was placed in the nave or chancel or in front of the pulpit.

In England, Henry VIII suppressed the great monasteries in 1539 and seized the wealth and treasures for the Crown. The income from the great Cathedral of Durham was given to Anne Boleyn. The Chantries Act caused further seizure of Church property. At the opening of Queen Elizabeth's reign the great rood and its figures of the Virgin, St. John, and the Crucifix were ordered taken down and destroyed, and the painting of the Doom on the tympanum was whitewashed, but the screen was left in place. In 1559 another edict cleared the churches of their medieval decorations such as pictures and images, and the only decorations officially allowed were stained-glass windows, the royal arms, and the tables of the Decalogue flanked by figures of Moses and Aaron. The Lord's Prayer and Creed, together with other scriptures, were also painted at the east end of the church, surrounded by angels and a glory of clouds with an "IHS." However, the medieval church plan with the three divisions was retained, although these traditional church buildings were not suited to the demands of the Prayer Book and congregational worship. To follow the English service it is necessary both to hear and to see what is done at the altar, and the compartmented church with its long chancel and screen dividing it from the nave cut off both the sight and sound of a service conducted at an altar in the far eastern end of the chancel. Many and various attempts were made to change and modify this medieval structure to meet the demands of the Prayer Book.

The Elizabethan communion table that replaced the fixed altar was allowed to be moved to suit the convenience of the service. Sometimes it was turned at right angles to the chancel wall, or it might be moved to the front of the chancel or even out into the nave. In some churches the altar was surrounded on all four sides by seats for communicants. There were attempts to move the font to the front of the church; but although this custom was adopted by the Lutherans and the Presbyterians, the Church of England usually kept the font at the entrance door "to signify that baptism was the entrance into the Church mystical." Attempts were also made to solve the problem of the pulpit and reading desk, and tall three-decker pulpits were erected in the center of the nave.

William Laud, Dean of Gloucester and later Archbishop of Canterbury, sought reforms in Church architecture that would return the dignity of the religious service by means of placing emphasis on the liturgy. The most important Laudian reform was the return of the altar to its position against the east wall. This emphasized the meaning and significance of the altar by giving it dignity and a place protected from confusion and irreverence. Altar rails were set up on three sides of the altar for protection, and the Laudian clergy then adopted the practice of having communicants kneel at the altar rail. During the years between 1617 and the Civil War there was considerable controversy about the position of the altar and other centers of worship, such as the pulpit and reading desk, before the church plan was finally clarified.

Although the medieval plan continued to influence church building, the seventeenth century architects were seeking a new type of church without a chancel screen. The first such church was St. Paul's, Covent Garden, designed by Inigo Jones in 1638. It was a single rectangular room with no screen division between the chancel and nave and no arcade aisles in the nave. The altar was set altarwise against the east wall. This room plan or auditory church was later popularized by Christopher Wren. In 1660, after the Great Fire in London, Christopher Wren was made surveyor general, and an important part of his work was to rebuild St. Paul's Cathedral and the London parish churches—fifty-one in all. His designs were classic in style, with domes and towers, pillars, arcades, and pediments.

The plan of St. Paul's Cathedral was similar to that of Norman and Gothic cathedrals. It had a nave, transepts with a chapel in either end, and a deep chancel, and was conventional in design except for the dome at the crossing of the transepts that formed a circular space. The proportions were fine, and the dramatic effect of light and shade produced a moving and devotional atmosphere. The dome was painted by James Thornhill with scenes from the life of St. Paul placed in a setting of painted arcades that repeats the lines of the pilasters of the drum. Grinling Gibbons' carvings of fruits and flowers in wood and stone decorate the choir stalls, the Corinthian capitals, and doorways, and the ironwork gates and window and sanctuary grille are by Jean Tijou. Architecturally, the building is a success, especially the dome, which is a masterpiece equal to St. Peter's in Rome. St. Paul's is Baroque translated into the English vernacular; but the Protestant architecture of the Reformation is generally conservative, and the classic style known as the Palladian is generally followed rather than that of the Baroque, which flourished only in Germany.

Wren's typical parish church was a room plan or auditory church designed so that the congregation not only could see but also hear the service. It had one room with benches or pews on either side of a center aisle, a three-decker pulpit, and an altar with rails against the eastern wall. A Wren church has three liturgical centers in an ascending scale of importance. By the door is the font; in the nave is the pulpit and reading pew; and against the east wall is the altar. Wren churches are small but wide in comparison to their length. They have fine proportion and purity of detail, dignity, and honesty and no undue dramatic effects. Although they are structurally plain, they are enriched with woodwork and plaster decoration, a coat of arms or urns on cornices and pediments. Communion rails are twisted or vase balusters that harmonize with the carved reredos and the black-and-white marble floor of the sanctuary, and form a solemn and dignified setting for the altar. The richest decoration is on the reredos and tall hexagonal pulpit set on a slender stem with sounding board above and circular staircase. The fault of Wren's churches from the ecclesiastical standpoint lay in the substitution of Gibbons' motifs of decoration for the traditional Christian symbolism. The imagery of the eternal was abandoned for such motifs as cherubs, fruit, and flowers, for art no longer had any formal significance in the Protestant ritual.

Architectural experiments concerning the pulpit and the reading desk continued during the seventeenth and eighteenth centuries. George Herbert, in the reconstruction of Leighton Bromswold, Huntingdonshire, placed the pulpit and reading pew or lectern at either side of the entrance to the chancel, where with variation they keep their dignified, balanced position today.

The destruction in the churches of Scotland was to a great extent due to the seizure by Henry VIII and the edicts of Elizabeth to "extinguish and destroy shrines, pictures, paintings and monuments of feigned miracles." Much of the church plate was carried off by the Catholic and Episcopal clergy. Some was given to influential families for safekeeping and some was sold for the repair of churches. In any case, the old church plate was not adaptable to the Reformed Church. The cup for the priest was not suitable for the congregation, and the pyx was not large enough. Much of the art that the Puritans later destroyed was not really old or good, but they did cause damage by turning the cathedrals into fortifications, and altars and images were destroyed or moved to the churchyard.

The old churches thus disrobed were used until the end of the seventeenth century. Then Puritan meetinghouses began to be built; but because there was little money the construction was simple, usually rectangular with a gallery. There was a pulpit with a sounding board that might have a carved dove with an olive branch at its center top. In addition, the pulpit might have carved cherub heads or fruit and flowers. The communion table was set in the nave, surrounded by an enclosure and benches. The Ten Commandments were usually painted on the east wall and flanked on either side by figures of Aaron and Moses. Though this austerity and bareness expressed the sobriety of the Scotch Reformed Church, it was brought about not only by the strictness of the teachings of the Church but also by the state of their finances.

But when the "temple is swept," dullness and ugliness creep in, and many Protestant churches were so absorbed with the search for Truth that they failed to see that Truth and Beauty go hand in hand. With the Reformation organized religion had turned against art for the first time in many centuries and denied its virtue or efficacy. The Protestant Church destroyed the art that religion itself had created and that had been one of its most potent agencies of operation.

* Lucas Cranach the Elder visualized the dogmatism of Luther. In addition to illustrating the Luther Bible and various Lutheran tracts with woodcuts, Cranach painted altarpieces in Lutheran Churches in Wittenberg, Weimar, Dessau, and Schneeberg. These altarpieces were painted under Luther's direction and portrayed Luther's guides to salvation—repentance and redemption through the cross of Christ. The cardinals and saints of Roman Catholic altarpieces are replaced by Luther, Melanchthon, and other Lutheran scholars. They are shown at the foot of the cross, baptizing, preaching, and even at the table of the Last Supper. Their chief interest is historical, and their value lies in the portraits of Luther and his family and followers and in the beautiful backgrounds of German landscape rather than in the aesthetic qualities of the compositions.

Notre-Dame de la Belle-Verrière. Window in south aisle of choir, Chartres Cathedral, twelfth century. *Archives Photographiques.*

Bronze baptismal font by Reiner von Huy, Church of St. Barthélemy, Liége, Belgium. *A.C.L., Bruxelles.*

The Garden of Eden from "Très Riches Heures" by the Limbourg brothers. Chantilly, fifteenth century. *Archives Photographiques.*

Opposite: Madonna and Child in polychromed oak. Ile-de-France, twelfth century. *Museum of Fine Arts, Boston.*

Apocalypse Tapestry, Angers: "And the fifth angel sounded, and I saw a star fall from heaven unto earth." – Revelation 9:1. *Archives Photographiques.*

Annunciation in a Gothic church (Sainte-Chapelle) shows details of architecture and large reliquary hanging over altar: J. Fouquet, "Livre d'Heures de St. Chevalier." Musée Condé, Chantilly. *Archives Photographiques.*

Below: Mérode Altarpiece by Robert Campin (1406-1444): the Annunciation, center panel. *Metropolitan Museum of Art, The Cloisters Collection.*

Paradise, from "The Garden of Earthly Delights," a triptych by Bosch in the Museo del Prado, Madrid. *Museo del Prado.*

Virgin and Child, by Giotto, from the Uffizi Gallery, Florence.
Photo Alinari.

The head of an ivory pastoral staff shows the perfection of Gothic carving. The curves of the figures of the Virgin and angels echo those of the structure of the lines of the staff in a swinging circular rhythm. France, fourteenth century. *Victoria and Albert Museum, London.*

A figure of Christ appearing to Mary Magdalene in the Garden, by Fra Angelico, Museo St. Marco, Florence. *Photo Alinari.*

"The Expulsion of Adam and Eve from Paradise," by Masaccio, in St. Maria della Carmine, Florence. The realistic figures express intense remorse, shame, and despair. *Photo Alinari.*

Baptistery door panel, Florence, by Ghiberti: Moses receives the Tablets of the Law. *Photo Alinari.*

“The Creation of Adam,” by Della Quercia: stone carving at doorway, St. Petronio, Bologna. The mighty rhythms of the figures suggest Michelangelo. *Photo Alinari.*

The bronze doors of St. Lorenzo, Old Sacristy, Florence, by Donatello. *Photo Alinari.*

"The Nativity," by Piero della Francesca. The contemplative beauty and repose of the figures express the quiet of holiness. Even the rhythmical joy of the angel choristers is static. The story is told with simplicity: there are no props, halos, or stars. *Trustees, National Gallery, London.*

Opposite: Botticelli's "The Nativity." The grace and rhythm of the dancing angels express the joy of the scene. In spite of the many ecstatic angels, the scene centers on the dominant figures set within the cave. *Trustees, National Gallery, London.*

Giovanni Bellini, "The Transfiguration." The landscape increases the quiet solemnity of the scene. *Photo Alinari.*

Giovanni Bellini, "The Madonna of the Pomegranate." The simplicity of composition and the attitude of the figures produce awe and reverence. *Trustees, National Gallery, London.*

Francesco Pesellino's devotional Crucifixion with St. Jerome and St. Francis. *National Gallery of Art, Washington, D.C., Samuel H. Kress Collection.*

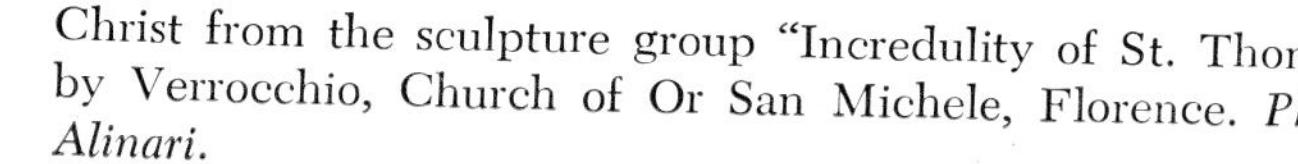

Christ from the sculpture group "Incredulity of St. Thomas" by Verrocchio, Church of Or San Michele, Florence. *Photo Alinari.*

Albrecht Dürer's "The Holy Family, with Three Hares." The heavenly throne becomes a grassy seat; the Christ Child busies Himself turning the pages of a book; and birds, animals, and German landscape form the background. *Metropolitan Museum of Art, Fletcher Fund.*

Matthias Grünewald, "The Risen Christ," right wing of the Isenheim Altarpiece, early sixteenth century. The circles of rainbow color follow early tradition, and by means of light we see the glory of God in the face of Jesus Christ. *Unterlinden Museum, Colmar.*

Patinir's "The Baptism." The landscape sets the spiritual message of the scene, and the real world of physical existence serves only to interpret the spiritual reality beneath. *Kunsthistorisches Museum, Vienna.*

Raphael's "The Alba Madonna," a triangular composition of figures set in space. *National Gallery, Washington, D.C.*

Leonardo da Vinci, "St. Anne with Virgin and Child," Louvre. The pyramidal composition is woven together by the lines of the figures. The idealized face of the Virgin is given added spirituality by the atmospheric effect of the landscape. *Archives Photographiques.*

Michelangelo, "The Creation of the Sun and Moon," Sistine Chapel, Rome. God is represented as an elemental force. *Photo Alinari.*

Caravaggio's "St. Sebastian," a dramatic use of light and dark. *Photo Alinari.*

"St. Teresa in Ecstasy," by Bernini, St. Maria della Vittoria, Rome. *Photo Alinari.*

Guido Reni's "The Assumption of the Virgin," an example of the melodramatic religious art that became sentimentalism when used by lesser artists. *Metropolitan Museum of Art, Wilbour Fund.*

PLATE XXXVIII

Opposite: The architecture of the Church of St. John Nepomuk, Munich, by the Asams, shows the turbulent forms of German Baroque. *German Tourist Information Office.*

Poussin's "The Holy Family." The placing of the figures, the landscape, and the relation of dark and light tones are composed with the express purpose of moving the emotions of the viewer. *Archives Photographiques.*

Opposite: El Greco, "The Agony in the Garden." *National Gallery, London.*

Rubens, "The Descent from the Cross." The Baroque use of diagonal composition and the undulating, tempestuous energy force the agony of the scene upon the spectator. *A.C.L., Bruxelles.*

PLATE XL

"The Last Supper," by Phillipe de Champaigne. The simplicity of the interpretation is reverent. *Archives Photographiques.*

"The Annunciation," Germanic Museum, Nuremberg, by Conrad Witz. The quiet beauty and austere simplicity give a Protestant interpretation to the theme. *Archives Photographiques.*

Rembrandt's "Christ with the Sick Around Him" ("The Hundred Guilder Print"). *Metropolitan Museum of Art, H. O. Havemeyer Collection.*

Rembrandt's "Christ Crucified Between the Two Thieves." The dramatic use of light concentrates on the Cross of Christ, while the details recede into shadows. The result is a great emotional theme, and the story episode becomes secondary. *Metropolitan Museum of Art, Gift of Felix M. Warburg and Family, 1941.*

St. Paul's Cathedral, London, by Sir Christopher Wren. *National Buildings Record.*

P. Saenredam, St. Bavo, Haarlem, the Netherlands. *National Gallery, London.*

PLATE XLIV

Interior of St. Paul's Chapel, New York City, one of the most beautiful examples of Georgian architecture still in existence in its original form. *From McClinton, "The Changing Church," Morehouse-Gorham.*

William Blake's "The Ancient of Days." The use of the compass as a symbol for the act of creation is derived from medieval manuscripts. *Whitworth Art Gallery, Manchester.*

PLATE XLVI

"Christ on the Cross," by Delacroix. The emotion is expressed by color and moving patterns of design. *Walters Art Gallery, Baltimore.*

Puvis de Chevannes, "St. Geneviève": a studied and intellectual expression by an idealist. *Archives Photographiques.*

"Christ Crowned with Thorns," by the sculptor F. Rude. Louvre Museum. *Archives Photographiques.*

Auguste Rodin, "St. John the Baptist." This is nineteenth century realism at its best. *Archives Photographiques.*

CHAPTER X

NINETEENTH CENTURY CHRISTIAN ART

It is not a Christian way of preaching if you preach Christ only in an historical manner; that is not to preach the glory of God.

—MARTIN LUTHER

The story of Christian art in the nineteenth century is more complicated than that of the preceding centuries. There is a deficiency of sources of research, for historians have generally ignored this period of bad art; also, the message of nineteenth century Christianity is not clear. In the antique periods there was a yearning for the other world, and thoughts of men were on the eternal. The art of the early Church was the joyful art of the Good Shepherd. Byzantine art expressed God's majesty and awe-inspiring qualities and the nonrational elements of Christianity. In Romanesque times there is still a yearning for the world of the spirit. The Gothic discovered nature and the life of this world, and expressed it in art with simple emotion. The charm of nature is also felt in the early Renaissance in the paintings of the van Eycks, in Dürer, and in Botticelli. These paintings are not descriptive, although they are based on Christian revelation. Instead they give the spirit of Christianity, not the letter, and their message is one of "Hallelujah" and "Te Deum." The Baroque period expressed ecstasy and sensual delight in religion, while the Reformation stressed the rational elements in Christianity, but also revealed a deep inward religious sentiment in such artists as Rembrandt. But from here on, the message of Christian art is not clear. The separation of the Church and art in the Protestant Church gave the artist his freedom, and each artist sought to express his own thoughts and ideas and to give his individual interpretation of Christian themes.

The religious art of the late Baroque returned to classic inspiration, as seen in the paintings of Poussin. Later in the century art became pictorial and picturesque—characteristics better suited to express the emotions of the middle class than the formal styles of Classic or Baroque. This light gracious style of the rococo, with its emphasis on beauty and frivolity, stands between the ceremonial Baroque period and the emotionalism of the romantic nineteenth century. Needless to say, there was little Christian art produced in the eighteenth century. Though Tiepolo painted great dome decorations in the Jesuit churches, the organization of the composition is gone, the movement is dispersed, and the figures float in space unrelated to the architectural scheme; the feeling of escape to the world of ecstasy is lost.

William Blake was the outstanding figure of a group of late eighteenth and early nineteenth century painters who included Henry Fuseli, Thomas Stothard, John Flaxman, and James Barry. Blake painted the sublime with greater vision and imagination. His subjects were scriptural but his content was spirit. In his own words he says: "I assert for My Self that I do not behold the Outward Creation." "When the Sun rises, do you not see a round disk of fire?" "Oh, no, no, I see an innumerable company of the Heavenly host crying 'Holy, Holy, Holy is the Lord God Almighty.' "

In this poetic imaginative spirit he painted such works as "When the Morning Stars Sang Together," "Jacob's Dream," "Ode to the Morning of Christ's Nativity," and the "Procession from Calvary." "God Creating Adam," "Nebuchadnezzar," and "Ancient of Days" are painted with as much imagination but more vigorous handling. His work has clarity of color and outline, although inspired by visions of eternity and infinity. Blake belonged to the great family of religious artists beginning with the early Christian and Byzantine. However, he was not accepted by the Church of his day, although his belief in the Gospel was the foundation of his whole life, thought, and art.

In France, Jean Jouvenet was the best-known painter of religious subjects at this time. The sculptors Jean Antoine Houdon, Jean Baptiste Lemoyne, and Edme Bouchardon also produced a few works in the religious field. Church architecture followed the Classic style, and such churches as La Madeleine and Saint-Sulpice were built in Paris. But the spirit of the age was expressed more accurately by the artists Jean Antoine Watteau, François Boucher, Jean Honoré Fragonard, and Jean Baptiste Greuze, who did not paint Biblical subjects.

During the years of the French Revolution there was also little art with religious subject matter. Classicism was the official style as exemplified by Jacques David and his pupil Jean Auguste Ingres, who stressed drawing and formal composition. Ingres painted classic Biblical scenes with little feeling, as did Pierre-Paul Prud'hon and Hippolyte Flandrin, who became the popular religious painter in France at this time. Flandrin painted cold, unemotional murals in churches; like the other artists of the period, he ignored the wealth of Christian emotion. Goethe says of the Classical Christian art of this era: "All Biblical pieces have been robbed of their truth and simplicity and spoilt by exaltation and austere ecclesiasticism. Stately mantles falling in folds make an effort to conceal the empty dignity of supernatural persons."

About this time, however, romanticism, hand in hand with a Catholic revival in France, increased the number of religious paintings and sculptures, and many new churches were built. Romanticism, coupled with realism, also thrived in Germany and England. It meant a change in outlook for art. There is escape into the past and escape into the future. In church architecture there were the Neoclassic and the Gothic revival, the Italianate and the Moorish. Architecture, in looking to the past for inspiration, catered to the people's love of the picturesque and the associational, their lack of aesthetic appreciation, and their understanding of correct imitation. Romantic writers directed attention toward a Gothic revival, and the Church hoped to rekindle the glories of medieval worship as well as of art and architecture. But the whole conception of church building changed. Church architecture no longer had a clear-cut style; instead it used past styles. In exploring many different styles it became superficial and lost its religious element and its organic quality. Even the Gothic revival had no real spiritual content.

In England many churches were built or reconstructed in the nineteenth century, and the whole program centered in the Neo-Gothic under the influence of Augustus Welby Pugin. Pugin not only designed the architecture of churches but also all the details of decoration, including hardware, lamps, altars, pulpits, and brass lecterns. He also designed articles for use in the service, such as candlesticks, chalices, tabernacles, and ceremonial vestments. His churches had hand-carved oak Gothic screens, floriated ornament stenciled on walls and ceilings, floriated Minton tilework on the floors, and tall stained-glass windows. Tall Gothic tabernacles centered the altars, which had six tall candlesticks, an embroidered frontal, dossal, and riddel curtains. There was too much color and there were too many accessories, but a perfection of detail and the dim light blended it all to a subdued richness.

Because Pugin's church plans included a chancel screen, an altar elevated on steps, altar lights, and Eucharistic vestments that the Church archaeologists were crusading for, Pugin had a great influence on nineteenth century church building in England. Christian archaeological societies, clergymen, and pious churchmen who controlled nineteenth century church building in England were more interested in the sacramental and liturgical aspects of the building than in the articulation of the architectural plan. With the publication of *Symbolism of Churches and Church Ornaments* (the translation of Durandus) by J. M. Neale and Benjamin Webb, church design became a matter of symbolism and Anglo-Catholic dogma rather than taste.

There had never been so many new churches built in England as in the years at mid-century—almost all were Gothic, and the majority of them were the work of hack architects. But toward the end of the century Ruskin's writings and the craft shops of William Morris and Sir Edward Burne-Jones and other late Pre-Raphaelites had considerable influence in improving the decoration of English churches. Paintings by George Frederick Watts, R.A.; Sir Frederick Leighton, Burne-Jones, and Sir William Reynolds-Stevens decorated churches built at this time. But churches built by the best-known architects, R. C. Carpenter, William Butterfield, Alexander Beresford-Hope, George Gilbert Scott, George Edmund Street, or John Dando Sedding, although a correct expression of the refined mediocrity of the people, are of social rather than aesthetic interest.

In Germany the great Cologne Cathedral was repaired and enlarged and an altarpiece was painted by Overbeck in 1854 (since removed), but the cathedral was not finished until the end of the nineteenth century. It is a mixture of medieval and nineteenth century Gothic, and was built around the famous Shrine of the Three Kings and the vast cathedral treasure of tabernacles, crosses, monstrances, chalices, and other works of devotional art made of gold and silver and set with enamels and precious stones. Gothic churches were also built at this time at Ulm, Munich, Trier, and other parts of Germany. In France churches were built in Gothic style under the direction of Eugène Viollet-le-Duc, who reconstructed and redecorated many of the great cathedrals and churches, such as Notre-Dame and the Saint-Chapelle.

In America meetinghouses and Congregational churches were built on classic lines, Roman Catholic churches in Lombard style, while Episcopalians usually chose Gothic. Wren's classic spires are prototypes of the New England churches. In New York City, Old St. Paul's was brick Georgian, but Trinity, Ascension, and Holy Communion, designed by Richard Upjohn in the mid-nineteenth century, were Gothic, as were Grace Episcopal and St. Patrick's Roman Catholic Cathedral, both designed by James Renwick.

The nineteenth century painter escaped to the Turkish and Oriental scene. In France, such artists as Joseph Vernet combined romanticism with realism and painted Biblical characters in Arab costume amid scenery that is archaeologically correct. Art no longer catered to religion or the monarch, but to the middle-class patron who wanted technical perfection. For the most part, individualism replaced the artist's social sense, and each artist expressed his own private world and created his own personal vocabulary in the great cycle of change wherein the artist freed himself of all outside restraints. The artist no longer sought to edify the soul but to speak to the heart of man. Thus, romanticism extended the scope of sixteenth century Humanism. Romanticism also brought back emotional painting, color, and the heavy brush stroke. Familiar things were made to serve the function of beauty, and this was all allied to native traditions and nationalism.

Since the beginning of the century, religion had become a favorite topic in Germany, and this visionary romantic talk of a return to old days when religion and art were in company inspired the German romanticists. A group of German romantic artists moved by reverence of early Roman Catholicism and primitive church painting, especially that of Fra Angelico, segregated themselves in a monastery near Rome. They called themselves Nazarenes. Friedrich Overbeck was the leader and the best painter of the group, which also included Peter von Cornelius, Wilhelm von Schadow-Godenhaus and Philipp Veit. Overbeck had a genius for masterly drawing, and his paintings have refinement and spirituality but are lacking in originality. His frescoes in the Marienkirche at Lubeck, and the cathedral at Cologne were long, tiresome sermons.

The Pre-Raphaelite movement in England toward the middle of the century was inspired by a similar combination of romantic emotion and piety. In the paintings of Dante Gabriel Rosetti religion and romance are entwined with poetry and symbolism to give a trancelike ecstasy and votive quality. The unique "Annunciation" and "The Girlhood of Mary Virgin" are the best known. Holman Hunt painted religious subjects with historical and archaeological accuracy but with labored religiosity, and his well-known "The Light of the World" is good allegory but not a great picture. Carlyle, visiting Hunt's studio when "The Light of the World" was on the easel, viewed the painting with distaste and criticized the Christ decked out in jeweled crown and kingly robes and compared it to Rembrandt's Christ, the Man of Sorrows, which Carlyle considered a true conception of the Christ of Christianity. Other Pre-Raphaelite painters were John Everett Millais, Ford Madox Brown, Arthur Hughes, and later George F. Watts, and Burne-Jones. The latter designed the mosaic decorations in the English church in Rome, Italy, which carry on the tradition of early mosaics. His ideas have originality and transcendental depths joined with scrupulous fidelity to nature.

The Pre-Raphaelites have gained high regard with Protestant churchmen, but the authority Clive Bell says: "The Pre-Raffaelites were men of taste who felt the commonness of the High Renaissance and the distinction of the Primitive. . . . They had the taste to prefer Giotto to Raffael. . . . They discovered in the primitives scrupulous fidelity to nature, superior piety, chaste lives. . . . How far they were from guessing the secret of primitive art appeared when they began to paint pictures themselves. Had the Pre-Raffaelites been blessed with profoundly imaginative minds they might have recaptured the spirit of the Middle Ages instead of imitating its least significant manifestations. But had they been great artists . . . they would have invented forms for themselves." Also according to Clive Bell, the Pre-Raphaelites, along with other nineteenth century artists, did not have sensibility to the profound significance of form or the power of creation—the secret of all great art. They were sincere but lacking in skill. The popularity of the Pre-Raphaelites stems from the fact that they were sincerely interested in religion and in the interpretation of the moral subject matter of the Bible that the nineteenth century clerics and middle-class devout public considered representative of Christianity. They painted no Crucifixions, no Passions, and no Temptations, but dwelt on rational Christianity with such works as "The Girlhood of Mary Virgin,"

"The Return of the Dove to the Ark," and "Christ in the House of His Parents." It takes a greater artist to interpret the Crucifixion than to paint a Good Samaritan, and it calls for a greater thinker to preach a sermon on the Transfiguration than on the subject of "love thy neighbor." The real truth lies in the fact that neither the nineteenth century artist nor the nineteenth century churchman could reach the heights of exalted thought. Perhaps the lesson is that religion no more bestows talent for the arts than it gives taste.

The French artist Eugène Delacroix was the greatest representative of nineteenth century romantic painting. He was a near genius amid a company of mediocre painters. Though his paintings have color, imagination, strength of expression, and dramatic action, he never reaches the imaginative depths of Rubens or Tintoretto. His religious paintings include the decoration of a chapel in Saint-Sulpice, Paris.

A few other nineteenth century artists who used religious subjects should be mentioned. Romanticism and realism were combined in the painting of Jean François Millet. Simplicity of form and volume, the elimination of detail, and the concentration on essential masses of light and dark mark him for a greatness he never achieved because of his reliance on ideas and symbols. Millet wrote of the Psalms: "They are my breviary. I get from them all that I do."

Jean Baptiste Corot, essentially a painter of landscape moods, sometimes uses silvery landscapes of dawn or twilight as the setting for such subjects as the Baptism of Christ, but although they are reverent in feeling they are idylls on the Christian theme in the same manner as the idyllic frescoes of Puvis de Chavannes, whose use of pale luminous color produces a peaceful and inspiring mood, and is excellent decoration. Joseph Turner painted water, air, and smoke in a way that expressed the ultimate reality of nature. Although his subject matter was never religious, he painted visions of the glory of God.

In Germany, artists of the Düsseldorf School, including Edward Steinle, painted religious subjects on the walls of many German churches, and such artists as Gabriel von Max, Eduard von Gebhardt, and Fritz von Uhde painted pictures with a social purpose and moral edification. These artists were for the most part good painters with originality, but they had no great depth. In their paintings Christianity becomes the gospel of the Kingdom of God on Earth, and Christ is no longer the "Man of Sorrows" and agony and torture, but the "Man of Galilee" who came to the lowly and the children, and healed the sick. This social gospel reflects the religious teaching of the late nineteenth century. It is human, tender, gentle, and mild. It is the gospel of kindness, courage, and brotherly love. It is also the moral gospel. In the paintings of von Gebhardt, Christ no longer wears a halo or a purple robe, but is shown in the costume of the Germans of the fifteenth century. Other artists went to Jerusalem or Damascus, and, seeing no red or blue robes, reclothed the Biblical characters in their own local costumes. But the costume and architecture of the East of the nineteenth century did not revive the inner spirit of the scene; and the pictures of these artists, although they contributed a new outlook to the Bible picture, produced realistic illustration just as James Tissot and Tarrant did some years later. This preoccupation with realism and historical accuracy suited the Victorians, but it had little to do with the essentials of Christianity.

However, Fritz von Uhde's Biblical characters clothed in the lowly costumes of the German peasant had a connection with the life of the times that gave his paintings an inner relationship to the Christianity of his age. These paintings have simplicity, tenderness, and quiet spiritual calm. Christ is represented as the brother of the people. He enters their humble houses, eats with them and blesses them, bringing hope and comfort, and the people reverence Him with bowed heads and pious gestures. There are light and atmosphere in the paintings, which are sincere, edifying, and original, but von Uhde has no great depth of religious feeling, although his paintings are in line with the Gospels and their moral force is influential.

The French painters Léon Lhermitte and Henri Lerolle also painted scenes among the lowly, and the Swiss painter Eugène Burnand painted sacerdotal scenes with a simplicity and reverence that interpreted the social gospel and the ministry of Christ. Other painters endeavored to create a devotional feeling with an atmosphere of legend. A group of later artists painted about religious feeling but not of it. They show religious processions and peasant women praying at a shrine or saying grace. Such sentimental pictures were popular and were a part of nineteenth century anecdote and genre painting.

The religious spectacular painting of the nineteenth century included such ostentatious creations as Mihály von Munkacsy's "Christ Before Pilate" and "Christ on Calvary." With dramatic realism, the figures are assembled as in the closing scenes of a grand opera. The whole gamut of human emotions is displayed with realism, but the paintings are illustration and have no deeper Christian content than a religious pageant. Such pictures were and are still sponsored by the clergy, and are also the sentimental delight of the average churchgoer, for our churches have been brought up on sentimentality and romanticism as far as art is concerned.

There is a progressive degeneration in nineteenth century Christian art until the last gasp is seen in works of washed-out realism and emotional sentimentality interpreted by mediocre artists. The goal of these artists was to represent accurately three-dimensional forms in two-dimensional space in such a way as to make them acceptable to the public "with anecdote and sentiment, telling a tale, pointing a moral, or cracking a joke, or touching a tender chord." This art, which was popular with the Church both then and now, is nothing more than Victorian chromo-photography. Nineteenth century "art was diseased," said Viollet-le-Duc.

Ecclesiastical sculpture of the nineteenth century seldom sank as low as painting, unless we include the makers of religious statuary. In the early nineteenth century Antonio Canova decorated tombs and monuments with classic angels and allegorical figures of great beauty. Their value is aesthetic rather than devotional, but Canova had great influence on nineteenth century sculptors, including the Danish sculptor Bertel Thorvaldsen, who is known in ecclesiastical circles for his marble statues of Christ and the Apostles in the Frauenkirche in Copenhagen. The severe classic architecture of the church, which is lined with pillars and arches set with statues of the Apostles, is a perfect setting for the larger-than-life figure of Christ set under pedimented columns at the east end of the church. But in spite of the impressive beauty and sincerity of the figure of Christ, there is a frigidity in the interpretation.

The sculpture exhibited in the British Exhibition of 1851 gave an excellent picture of the state of religious sculpture at that date. The French sculptor François Rude exhibited the head of Christ. Rude was well known for his religious figures, which included a bronze Crucifixion and Virgin de Douleur for the Church of St. Vincent de Paul, an Immaculate Virgin for the Church of St. Gervaise, a Baptism of Christ in the Church of the Madeleine, and a bust of Christ Crucified now in the Louvre. Rude's sculpture combines classic line with emotion and dramatic feeling. However, the general characteristics of the romantic realistic nineteenth century sculpture are more apparent in the titles of the other pieces of religious sculpture shown at the British Exposition, which included "David with the Head of Goliath," "Prodigal's Return," "Rebecca at the Well," "The Finding of Moses," and the sentimental "Children Kissing the Cross." The last title, especially, reveals the sad storytelling state to which Christian sculpture had sunk at this time.

Realistic sculpture, which reached its height of expression in Bernini's St. Theresa, had become so realistic in the nineteenth century that the technical competence of the sculptor and his skillful representation became the ideal of sculpture. But the realistic mode is not suited to higher levels of thought, and the shortcomings of realism are revealed in symbolic or religious subjects in which the idea or content is of more importance than the physical appearance. The perfect rendering of the physical appearance detracts our attention from the beauty and depth of feeling of such work even in the hands of sculptors as great as Constantin Meunier or Auguste Rodin, who, with a few others, stand out from the general run of nineteenth century artists.

Rodin was the final figure in the nineteenth century march of realistic sculpture. But such was his genius and universal outlook that he transcended realism to become one of the great sculptors of all time. His sculpture has profound conception of subject matter and dramatic expression of human emotions. His greatest project, "The Gate of Hell," included many of his well-known figures, such as "The Thinker." "The Prodigal Son" is a dramatic expression of repentance, and "John the Baptist" has power and stark realism, while the symbolic hands called "The Cathedral" are a combination of symbol and reality.

Another nineteenth century sculptor of great genius was the American Augustus Saint-Gaudens. He is best known for his work on monuments, although he designed some sculpture for churches, including "The Adoration of the Angels" around the cross in St. Thomas's Church, New York City. The memorial to Phillips Brooks at Trinity Church, Boston, included a head of Christ, but the most outstanding work of Saint-Gaudens was the mourning figure on the Adams Monument in Rock Creek Cemetery, Washington, D.C. The mysterious profundity and unearthly calmness and serene repose of the figure make it one of the great pieces of Christian sculpture.

The Roman Catholic Church of the nineteenth century allowed the use of cheap plaster toy-shop saints, paper flowers, tinsel, and chromo-lithographs to produce a sort of folk-art atmosphere that was near and dear to the people. There were also cheap Virgin Marys enthroned in roses, and blood-trickling Sacred Hearts that are gaudy and lacking in inspiration. The Protestant Church rejected these tawdry things, but while she whitewashed her walls and swept her temple clean, she accepted the dreamy-eyed veiled Virgin of "The Annunciation" by Arthur Hacker and the scent of roses and violets in melodramatic Madonnas of William Bouguereau, who, with their large eyes covered by sensuous drooping lids, were sisters to his nymphs and goddesses. The Protestant Church also rejected the harshness of the crucifix and the Man of Sorrows, but accepted the sentimental, weak, unreal Christs of Ary Scheffer, Plockhorst, and Hofmann which do not correctly interpret the person of Christ or the truths of the Bible. These popular painters have robbed Christ of His strength and made Him a sweet, poetic nineteenth century aesthete. There is no "glory of God in the face of Jesus Christ." In the interpretation of Bible stories and Gospel truths, these sentimental artists substituted scenes of illustrative realism for depth of feeling and devotion. They portray the scenes and illustrate the stories of the Bible, but do not infuse the spirit or atmosphere of Christianity. There is no mystic quality, no glory, no exaltation, and no hieratic significance. They are at one and the same time false and shallow Christianity, and degraded art. They give unreality and pious edification, but no real devotion. They imitate but do not convince.

Even the best nineteenth century Christian art stopped short of the greatest art because its interpretation was based on moral and theological doctrines. The artist is preaching a sermon rather than giving the spirit and atmosphere of religion not sacrificed to any creed. He has forgotten the value of space, light, air, clouds, vastness, and silence. Most of the artists whose pictures are used in religious education today date from this period. They are not even mentioned in histories of art or known in the art world. They were just among the number of hundreds of artists who took their ounce of talent seriously, and their dedication to art was greater than their abilities. Ruskin's words in *Modern Painters* about mediocre Christian art apply today as they did when he wrote them in the nineteenth century:

"The group calling themselves Evangelical ought no longer to render their religion an offence to the men of the world by associating it only with the most vulgar forms of art. It is not necessary that they should admit either music or painting into religious service; but if they admit either the one or the other, let it not be bad music nor bad painting: it is certainly in nowise more for Christ's honor that His praise should be sung discordantly or His miracles painted discreditably, than that His word should be preached ungrammatically."

Yet, although nineteenth century Christian art was mediocre, it gave a fresh approach to the life of Christ. The Church art of past ages had been doctrinal and ecclesiastical. Since it was painted to the order of the Church, there were traditional scenes of the story of Christianity from the Old Testament and the life of Christ in such subjects as the Annunciation, the Nativity, the Journey to Jerusalem, the Last Supper, and scenes of the Passion, the Crucifixion, Resurrection and Ascension. Art also illustrated the doctrine of the Incarnation and Atonement, and gave us Pietàs and Madonnas for devotional worship. But the nineteenth century artist changed all this. He was working for his own expression, not to the order of the Church; thus he shunned doctrines and chose human relationships to express his own insights and aspirations.

Themes from the lives of the Old Testament characters that tell of their human life rather than of the great experiences that link them with Christianity's dogmas were popular. In fact, this is one reason for the popularity of nineteenth century art with the clergy and Christian teachers, because in the themes of nineteenth century artists they find stories of events and minor episodes of the Bible that were seldom portrayed in the great ages of Christianity. From the Old Testament, such subjects as Elijah in the Wilderness, Moses Before Pharaoh, Tamar and Absalom, Delilah, the Death of Moses, and Ruth and Boas are available in nineteenth century art. The New Testament was interpreted by scenes from the childhood and ministry of Christ and the lives of the Disciples.

Earlier, there were few scenes of the boyhood of Christ. In the nineteenth century He was portrayed in His father's carpenter shop and in the temple. He was shown with children as a teacher, as a companion in the house of Mary and Martha, in the peasant's lowly home, and with the adulteress. He was painted as healing the sick and raising the daughter of Jairus as well as Lazarus, and He is shown talking to Nicodemus, knocking at the door, walking through the wheat fields, in the garden, and mourning over the city. These are all Protestant themes and relate to a practical, rational religion rather than to the nonrational and mystic. As valuable as they are in teaching religion, such incidents do not have the broad universal scope of the great themes of Christianity, nor do they have the power of inspiration for the artist; and herein lies much of the failure of nineteenth century Christian art.

But the basic faults of nineteenth century Christian art are more fundamental. The isolation of the arts that began in the eighteenth century is now accomplished. Each art—architecture, sculpture, painting—sought to be complete in itself. Thus, there is no unified style, and the church building is no longer a composite work of art. The anaemic religious painting of the period had no connection with the architecture, and though the sculpture was attached to the building it was not incorporated into the building plan and design. But the prime reason for the decline of nineteenth century religious art was the lack of a Christian iconography. Since the picture was no longer needed as an instrument of worship, the clergy refused much of the art of the past, but failed to provide a new iconography of art for the present.

CHAPTER XI

CONTEMPORARY CHURCH ART

> *Only a cathedral spire can show us a point in the sky where our soul is suspended! In the disquietude of the night the stars seem to show us points of hope in the sky; this immobile spire also indicates to us an endless number of them. It is these points in the infinite which are precursors of the new art: to draw in space.*
>
> —JULIO GONZÁLEZ, *Sculptor*

While Church artists and architects were still concerned with the rebirth of art styles based on the past, a new style was brought into being by the secular artists and architects of Germany and France. Significant buildings were built in new forms with contemporary materials, and in painting and sculpture masters of impressionism and expressionism were producing art of a high quality. Many of these artists used religious subject matter, but no place was found in the Church for the great painting and sculpture of the period. Instead, from the outset of modern artistic movements the Church ignored contemporary art and made use of second-rate art that harked back to the past.

The twentieth century revival in Christian art and architecture also began in the nineteenth century, but it did not develop from the inspiration of the new art styles or from the different materials of construction but rather from a new spirit within the Church itself, called the Liturgical Movement. The Liturgical Movement began in the Roman Catholic Church in the revival of Benedictine monasticism at the Abbey of Solesmes in France and in the restoration of the Gregorian chant. The work was enlarged in scope at the monasteries of Beuron and Maria Laach in Germany to include the revival of liturgical art. The real purpose of the Liturgical Movement was to return to the basic principles of Christian worship and to allow the worshiper an active part in the Eucharistic service. To do so, it was necessary for the worshiper to see as well as hear, and the task of the Church was to evolve a church architecture that united the congregation as nearly as possible with the altar. To accomplish this the space had to be cleared and all screens and impediments to seeing the service removed. The reredos was dispensed with. The simple altar stood out from the wall in plain view of all the people, and unnecessary statues and side altars were done away with.

The Anglican and Lutheran churches also engaged in the liturgical renaissance to a certain extent, as well as the nonliturgical churches, including the Church of Scotland. Among those who contributed new ideas in church planning and decoration, besides the Benedictine monks of Maria Laach and Romano Guardini, were Alexandre Cingri in Switzerland and Father Pie Régamey and the artists Maurice Denis and Georges Desvallières, who formed a workshop for church decoration in France; and by the 1930's the sculptor Eric Gill and a group of artists were doing contemporary stone carvings and frescoes in English Roman Catholic and Protestant churches. The first new type of church was Notre-Dame de Raincy, built near Paris in 1923 by the architect Auguste Perret. Many similar churches were built in Germany and Switzerland, including St. Anthony at Basel, designed by Karl Moser; the Blessed Sacrament at Aachen, designed by Rudolf Schwarz; and St. Engelbert, Cologne, by Dominicus Böhm. Contemporary ecclesiastical architecture has developed through the influence of the design of these pioneer churches and their variation of the use of the circle and rectangle and circle and triangle.

Contemporary church architecture has liberated itself from traditional forms and ornaments. The steeple and the spire have been replaced by the circle of the universe, the star shape of the heavens, and the fish shape of early symbolism, but the purpose in most cases is practical rather than symbolical. Some new forms, such as the Chapel of Notre-Dame du Haut, Ronchamp, and the chapel of the study center for Dominicans in Lyon, France, by Le Corbusier, are poetic expressions of sculptural architecture. We see the spirit of the times echoed in these contemporary churches, the desire for light and open space, for simplicity and order, and for the warmth and intimacy of community worship and shelter. Spiritual concentration is achieved through severely ascetic forms. The change in present-day church architecture has also been influenced by the complexities of modern church functions, the high cost of building the old styles, and the disappearance of dedicated craftsmen as well as the changing techniques of building. But a deeper and more compelling search for man's knowledge of himself, the universe, and God seeks new ways of expression.

The determining factor in the interior plan is the position and importance of the altar. Architects broke away from the traditional position of the altar at the eastern end of the church. It was moved out from the wall and even placed in the center of the church for greatest prominence. The effect of color and lighting, as well as position, was employed to emphasize the altar. Glass domes and windows and artificial lighting are all used to focus the light on the altar. In one of his earliest churches, Rudolf Schwarz at Aachen advanced liturgical thinking by his severe contrasts of dark and light. A black marble altar is placed within a setting of bare white walls. Two rows of windows in the sanctuary give light to put emphasis on the altar. There is no statuary, and the artificial lighting consists of thin lines of fluorescent light multiplied in strength according to the importance of the service. One undivided space embraces both altar and congregation. The people see and hear, and the liturgy becomes the decoration of the church. Everything that is not concerned with the Mass is relegated to a subsidiary hall.

There is no place in the contemporary church for the traditional use of sculpture and painting. The altar restored to its table form has no need for reredos or altarpiece, and pillars and side chapels have also been done away with. Art has again become a part of the worship rather than the decoration of the church. For this reason it is important that the subject matter of the art—painting, sculpture, glass, or mosaic—used in the sanctuary relate to the sacraments at the altar rather than to the history of the Church. In the Roman Catholic Church the crucifix is the only image the rubrics require, but most churches also have an image of the Mother of God. The images of the saints, so numerous in churches since the seventeenth century, have been moved from their central position in the contemporary church in order to concentrate attention on the altar. In ancient times images were used as reliquaries, and their central position was permissible because of their religious significance as well as their part of the artistic whole. Although there are no longer so many figures of saints, there is still much work in the church for the artist. The altar itself is an important theme for art. Even the plainest altar is a problem in sculptured form and demands the assistance of an artist to define its proportions and form. It, as well as the ciborium or canopy, may also require the work of a painter, sculptor, or mosaicist for ornament, and in order to make full use of the colors and surface qualities of the various materials. The preferred shape of the altar is now a chest or slab or table with columns and arches. Beauty is achieved by fine proportions rather than by applied ornamentation. Henri Matisse at Vence set a simple slab of granite on a massive column. The base of the contemporary altar is sometimes a figure, or the altar slab may be set on a chest. The chest type of altar may have suitable sculpture or mosaic decoration. In the Church of Our Lady at Trier Rudolf Schwarz placed a simple chest on an arched base in the center of the church. The altar of the Cathedral of St. Bavon in Haarlem has screens of bronze between the four marble columns that hold the altar slab. The font also requires the service of a craftsman or sculptor. The contemporary font is simple and architectural in design. Where space permits, the bowl itself, rather than the base or cover, is the important part of the structure, and here the decoration is concentrated. Simple utilitarian fonts in complete harmony with the architecture have been designed.

Articles of liturgical significance, such as candlesticks, cross or crucifix, sanctuary lamp, tabernacle, chalice, pyx, and ciborium, require the service of the artist-craftsman and silversmith if there is to be the proper unity and beauty of design and harmony with the altar and the organic design of the architecture. Today the Church is turning from the commercial machine-made object of liturgical usage, and in the desire for greater reverence in all articles used at the altar the Church seeks the skill, imagination, and careful handling of the artist-craftsman. The silversmith and goldsmith with artistic genius, as well as fine craftsmanship, are in great demand. In Europe the outstanding artists and craftsmen are again employed by the Church. Significant crucifixes and other religious images have been made.

A brief survey of contemporary Church art in the various countries of Europe and in America will show that many fine artists and craftsmen are now doing Church work throughout the world. In the first twentieth century modern churches there was little sculpture, painting, or mosaic except in Our Lady of the Trinity at Blois, where the façade was sculptured by the brothers Martel. In the interior there are Stations of the Cross by Lambert-Rucki and mosaics and glass by L. Barillet. In the Church of Our Lady of Grace at Assy in 1950 the architect Maurice Novarina, together with Father Couturier, planned the art work and employed the famous contemporary artists Georges Rouault, Alfred Manessier, Fernand Léger, Germaine Richier, Georges Braque, Jacques Lipchitz, Marc Chagall, Henri Matisse, Jean Bazaine, and Jean Lurçat to design the mosaics, glass, crucifix, and tapestry that decorate the church. Léger and Bazaine also did the painting, glass, and mosaics at Audincourt in collaboration with the architect Novarina. Lambert-Rucki, Barillet, Gabriel Loire, Jean Cocteau, Jacques Villon, Chavignier, Dodeigne, Idoux, Chesnay, and Leon Zack are other well-known artists who have designed works of art for contemporary churches in France. At Vence, Matisse not only planned the architecture but designed the glass, tile, painting, and sculptured crucifix, as well as the vestments, to create the chapel as a composite work of art. Jean Cocteau recently decorated the old Romanesque Chapel of St. Peter in Villefranche-sur-Mer with contemporary frescoes that illustrate the life of St. Peter, the fisherman. Albert Gleizes painted an abstract fresco in a church at Chantilly, and Braque decorated the Chapel of St. Dominique at Varengéville. Chagall, who decorated the small baptistery in the church at Assy, has also designed a series of prints that illustrate the Bible. The use of color to express spiritual and emotional moods accents the melancholy and suffering of his paintings and relates him to contemporary Christian art expression.

Rouault is the greatest religious painter of our time, and his work has had great influence upon contemporary Church art, especially stained glass. As a boy he worked on stained-glass windows, and because of this early training his paintings have simplicity and force, pure intense color, and heavy black outlines that give them the hieratic grandeur of primitive Christianity, yet his originality breaks with the past. Though Rouault's paintings are realistic, they seem abstract because only essential and significant elements are expressed. He deforms the body of Christ to express divine Passion and human cruelty and to show the majesty of suffering. The primitive concept of Christian art had been heralded by the German expressionist Emil Nolde, who painted his religious feeling with violent form, emotional color, and a heavy bold technique. Such paintings of his as "Pentecost," "The Last Supper," and "Christ Among the Children" give the spirit of the Bible but were ignored by the Church until recent years.

In Germany such well known sculptors as Ewald Mataré, Ernst Barlach, Gerhard Marcks, Hein Wimmer, Kurt Schwippert, Elmar Hillebrand, and others designed sculpture for baptismal fonts, altars, figures for church exteriors, Stations of the Cross, processional crosses and tabernacles in bronze. When the Cologne Cathedral was reconstructed after the bombing, the contemporary sculptors Eduard Bell, Erlefried Hoppe, and others designed the figures that replaced the destroyed Gothic statues. This same mingling of the old and new is seen in the reconstruction of many bombed German churches. Joseph Jaekel designed a contemporary bronze cock for St. Marienkirche zu Oberhausen in the Rhineland, and Ewald Mataré designed a bronze doorway and angel for a church in Essen. The bronze door of Der Kloster Kirche in Brühl, Cologne, with modern symbols of the Old and New Testaments, was designed by Elmar Hillebrand. Silver liturgical articles such as chalices, monstrances, and crosses are designed by Tom Rückel, Fritz Schwerdt, Adelmar Dölger, O.S.B.; Karl Schrage, Wilhelm Polders, and Hermann Jünger, who designed the gold tabernacle for the chapel at the Brussels Fair. Painting does not take such an important place as sculpture, but in Würzburg, Germany, the architect Hans Schädel collaborated with painter Georg Meistermann, and the painting on the east wall of the church sets the mood of the service.

In Switzerland art in the church is also beginning to be of importance. Léger has designed concrete-glass windows at Courfaive, and in a church at Thayngen the sculptor Josef Rickenbacker has designed a contemporary "Last Supper" and sculptured the base of the altar. Often the wall behind the altar is filled with stained glass, a mural, or a tapestry. Although Swiss contemporary churches are simple and functional, the articles of liturgical usage, such as vestments and goldsmiths' work, are outstanding in design and workmanship.

Ecclesiastical goldsmiths include Klaus Brodman, Alex Schaffner, and Meinrad Burch-Korrodi who more than anyone has set the trend of functionalism and simplicity in the design of present-day objects of liturgical usage. Their crosses, candlesticks, monstrances, and reliquaries stand on sturdy bases. The design of the monstrance accentuates the form of the wafer, and the chalice shape is simple and balanced, although it may be adorned with cabachon jewels and enamel. The weaver Sr. Augustina M. Flüeler and Erna Schillig who appliqués vestments are known throughout the world for their original contemporary designs.

In Holland the outstanding silversmith and designer of liturgical art and church decoration is Jan-Eloy and Leo Brom of Utrecht.

In Belgium there is a renaissance of religious art centering in the monasteries at the Abbey of Maredsous near Namur, Belgium. The altar has been moved to the center of the sanctuary, and a low-ceilinged structure of contemporary design makes a shelter within the vast Gothic church that draws the worshipers together near the altar. Shrines, votive candlestands, and statues have been banished, and the polychrome decorations of the nineteenth century have been hidden under a coating of gray paint. All articles of liturgical use are of functional contemporary design, being designed and made in the Ecole des Métiers d'Art, which is at the abbey. The influence of this workshop is seen in other abbeys and churches of Belgium, including the Abbey of St. André near Bruges. In other churches in Belgium and Germany the plaster gingerbread of the Baroque is being scraped off to reveal the original stone and architectural simplicity of the churches' Gothic structure. The action of the abbeys has also been decisive in the modernization of Church vestments and religious objects of all sorts. Michel Martens is known for contemporary designs in stained glass. Talented painters and designers are again working in the tapestry industry, and tapestries with religious subject matter by Jan Yoors and others are being made for churches. The old art of Dinant copperwork has been revived with the aid of the prominent sculptor Oscar Jespers and the new forms and ideas of the Benedictine monks of the Abbey of Maredsous. The religious work of the goldsmiths and silversmiths of Belgium has been important down through the centuries, and today the enamels of Odette Grégoire and the metalwork of F. Jacques and Marcel Wolfers and Bonduel is equal to the greatest. Hand-woven, embroidered, and appliquéd vestments are made at the abbeys in the vicinity of Namur where the painter J. M. Londot and the sculptor J. Williams have also done contemporary church work.

Contemporary church art in Italy centers in the large industrial cities, particularly Milan and Bologna, where the growth of the city demanded new churches. By modern use of lighting and space, these contemporary churches have the appearance of paleo-Christian basilicas, and the best of them include seats for pious meditation and an altar setting with an effect of mystic exaltation. Sculpture, fresco, and mosaic are employed in their decoration. Since they are Roman Catholic, statues, crucifixes, and other sacral furnishings are needed. Many nationally known sculptors, including Giacomo Manzu, Luciano Minguzzi, Marino Marini, Mario Negri, Pericle Fazzini, Virginio Ciminaghi, Emilio Greco, and Francesco Messina, have designed statues, baptismal fronts, and bronze doors for contemporary Italian churches. Manzu executed a series of low reliefs in bronze, including Stations of the Cross, a bronze door for St. Peter's in Rome, and incidents of the Passion with references to the contemporary scene, such as a debauched German officer at the Crucifixion and a cardinal at the Deposition. Other sculptors who have done work in contemporary churches include Attilo Nani, Franco Lombardi, Pio Semproni, Biagio Poidimani, Nicola Sebastio, and Arrigo Minerbi, who designed a new bronze door for the Cathedral of Milan. Fresco painters and mosaicists working on modern Italian churches include Fiorenzo Tomeo, A. Mori, Gigiotti Zanini, Bruno Cassinari, and the well-known painter Carlo Carrà. With the vast amount of Renaissance tradition so near at hand, it is not strange that only the most original Italian artists are contemporary in their outlook.

In England church architecture was slow to take on the contemporary style. Instead there was a striving to modernize the Gothic and Baroque by means of color and simplicity and a trend for originality in decoration within a traditional plan. Churches were stripped and streamlined. Then the war put an end to all church building and left the country with demolished and damaged churches. In the process of rebuilding, England has awakened to the changed atmosphere and the new demands of the present-day church. Sir Edward Maufe designed a contemporary cathedral for Guilford, a Jacob Epstein figure of Christ in Majesty was put on an arch in the nave of Llandaff Cathedral at Cardiff, Wales, and the reconstruction of St. Matthew's Anglican Church in Northampton includes a Madonna and Child by Henry Moore and a Crucifixion by Graham Sutherland. But the most important contemporary church in England is Coventry Cathedral, which is rising from the ruins of the old Gothic Church of St. Michael. The structure of pierced reinforced concrete, as contemporary as any twentieth century church, incorporates the old Gothic tower and spire. Beside the main entrance is a sculpture by Sir Jacob Epstein, "Wings of

Triumph," which shows a mighty St. Michael victorious over the Devil. In the interior of the cathedral Graham Sutherland has designed a tapestry for the wall behind the altar. The glass screen between the narthex and the nave is etched with religious figures by the well-known artist John Hutton. The font is topped by a lacy metal structure of contemporary abstract design, and the stained-glass windows by Keith New, John Piper, Lawrence Lee, and Geoffrey Clarke are given sacred significance by the emotional use of color. The vestments are being designed by John Piper, and cross and candlesticks are by Robert Goodden and Geoffrey Clarke.

The exhibition of the British Artists Craftsmen circulated in America in 1959–1960 was an indication that the British craftsman is using religious subject matter and that the British Church of today is interested in the work of these artist craftsmen, for much of the work of the best-known artists of Britain is concerned with church decoration. John Hutton, Geoffrey Clarke, John Piper, Keith New, Patrick Reyntiens, and Margaret Traherne have executed stained glass for many churches, including Coventry Cathedral. Henry Moore and Sir Jacob Epstein have sculptured Madonnas and figures of Christ for several English churches, and F. E. McWilliam, Robert Clatworthy, Robert Adams, Bernard Meadows, and Barbara Hepworth have also executed sculpture with religious subject matter. Geoffrey Clarke and Leslie Thornton have made metalwork Stations of the Cross, crucifixes, and candelabra for churches; and the silversmiths Gerard Benney, Dunstan Pruden, Alexander Styles, and others have designed altarpieces and eucharistic silver. Contemporary vestments are being designed by Margaret Traherne, John Piper, Ann Bruce, Margaret Kaye, and Thea Somerlatte, while many skilled embroideresses are also working on contemporary church vestments. Among English painters, Stanley Spencer concerned himself with religious subjects, personal and unconventional in their interpretation, including "The Nativity" and "The Last Supper." Graham Sutherland paints the Christ of his Crucifixion as an image of neglect, a Christ suffering on the Cross for many years. Sutherland's portrait of Christ in Majesty with the Evangelist has been woven into the tapestry for Coventry Cathedral, and such paintings as "Oracle," "Thorn Cross," and "Thorn Cross in Oval" also are of religious inspiration.

Perhaps the outstanding Christian work of art of the twentieth century is Jacob Epstein's "Ecce Homo." This powerful Christ with immense hands, shoulders, chin, and a wreath of thorns compels by means of its monumental simplicity. This Christ is austere, "having no form or comeliness," and stands sullen and stern, accusing the world and asking, Why? Epstein says of his "Ecce Homo": "My statue of Christ stands and accuses the world for its grossness, inhumanity, cruelty, and beastliness, for the First World War and for later wars in Abyssinia, China and Spain, which culminated in the Second World War."

In the late nineteenth century and early twentieth century three American architects, Henry Hobson Richardson, Louis H. Sullivan, and Frank Lloyd Wright, were pioneering a new architecture related to the American scene. Although they were not primarily church architects, the few churches that each of them designed were unique and forward thinking, and helped set the pattern for the future of American church architecture. Richardson had broken the shackles of Gothic in his epoch-making Trinity Church in Boston, which was Romanesque in inspiration but conceived with honesty and vitality. It set a new fashion in church planning that met the broadening social conscience of twentieth century Church thinking, but it retained the mystery, quiet, and awe that lead to worship. Burne-Jones designed the windows, and John La Farge painted the mural decorations. La Farge's later murals in the St. Thomas Church and the Church of the Ascension, New York City, revived the art of mural decoration in America. La Farge also designed stained glass for Columbia University Chapel and other churches. Louis C. Tiffany was also active in church decoration, designing stained glass, textiles, and articles of liturgical usage in motifs related to Art Nouveau. He exhibited a completely furnished chapel in the World Columbian Exposition of 1893, and a complete Tiffany chapel, the Wade Memorial Chapel at Lakeview Cemetery, Cleveland, Ohio, remains intact today with its superb stained-glass window depicting "The River of Life." Louis H. Sullivan, the creator of the skyscraper office building, was also antitraditional in his church designs, as evidenced in the original form and details of St. Paul's Methodist Episcopal Church, Cedar Rapids, Ohio. The severe regularity of its windows, the block-like tower, and the square doorway express the puritanism of Methodism. As early as 1887 Frank Lloyd Wright set a native style of church design in his shingled Unitarian Chapel in Sioux City, Iowa, and later, in 1906, he further defined his modern cubist construction in Unity Church,

Oak Park, Illinois. In 1950 Wright designed First Unitarian Church, Madison, Wisconsin, with a folded roof structure and a peak meant to represent hands raised in prayer. In the triangular diamond-shaped interior the use of natural light and native materials relates to Wright's prairie-type architecture.

But American taste in religious art and architecture was so centered in the traditional past, and particularly in the Gothic, that these new and original ideas of American architects and artists were for the most part ignored, while church people slumbered in the romantic sentimentality of nineteenth century medievalism. This architectural escapism dominated the thinking of both the clergy and the people, and resulted in the building of Gothic churches that harked to the past. In the first third of the twentieth century, many Episcopal churches were built in the formal medieval manner, but with daring eclecticism and originality, by the firm of Cram, Goodhue and Ferguson. Vast sums were spent on elaborately carved doorways, stone reredos, carved wooden choirstalls, and font covers, as well as pulpits, lecterns, sedilia, and liturgical furnishings such as altar crosses, candlesticks, chalices, and alms basins all "wrought" with Gothic detail and symbolism. The greatest of these churches were St. Thomas, St. Vincent Ferrer, the Chapel of the Intercession, and the Cathedral of St. John the Divine in New York City. Washington Cathedral, Heavenly Rest, and Riverside Church in New York, and Kirk in the Hills, Birmingham, Michigan, were built some years later.

Byzantine-Romanesque architecture was revived in the Episcopal Church of St. Bartholomew, New York City, and recently in the Roman Catholic cathedrals at Baltimore and Washington. Although all these churches have elements of beauty, they hark to the past. In most cases, the stained glass is of excellent quality, designed and made abroad or by the outstanding masters of stained glass in America, notably Lawrence Saint, D'Ascenzo, Willet, Burnham, Reynolds, and Connick. The religious murals in the Ralph Adams Cram churches were painted by Sister Mary Veronica, an Episcopalian nun, and the materials for the dossals and altar frontals were designed and woven by the Talbots of Philadelphia. The best-known sculptors of America were employed to design figures for the doorways and carved stone reredos, pulpits, and lecterns. These figures, consistent with the spirit of the architecture and traditional in iconography, are original in conception and execution.

A large number of sculptors in America are known for their religious figures and for many years have been busy working on commissions for churches and memorials. Notable among these sculptors were and are John Angel, Gutzon Borglum, Lee Lawrie, Gleb Derujinsky, Jean de Marco, Donald de Lue, Ivan Mestrovic, Pietro Montana, Theodore Barbarosa and Leo Friedlander. Early in the twentieth century the sculptor Frederick MacMonnies did three bronze angels for St. Paul's Chapel, New York City; bronze doors were made by Charles Niehaus, Karl Bitter, and J. Massey Rhind for Trinity Church, and the sculptors Herbert Adams, Philip Martiny, and Andrew O'Connor designed bronze doors and architectural sculpture for St. Bartholomew's Church. St. Patrick's bronze doors were designed by Andrew O'Connor, and Isidore Konti did the doors of Grace Church. John Angel, Lee Lawrie and Saint-Gaudens designed sculpture for the new St. Thomas Episcopal Church while John Angel, M. M. Swartzott, Gutzon Borglum, and many others did sculpture for the Cathedral of St. John the Divine and the Chapel of the Intercession in New York City. Many well-known figure sculptors are now working on commissions for the large, traditional Roman Catholic Churches being built in Washington, D.C., and Baltimore.

There are other sculptors who design religious figures in a simplified modern vein, yet are acceptable to the conservative clergy and churchgoer. Among these are Alfeo Faggi, Janet de Coux, George Kratina, Henry Kreis, Moissaye Marans, Henry Rox, and Carl Schmitz. William Zorach and Jose de Creeft and Oronzio Maldarelli are also known for sacred figures in a modern simplified style. There are also contemporary sculptors such as Charles Umlauf and Calvin Albert who work for contemporary church architects, although their work is accepted with reluctance by some churchgoers.

A new era in church building in America began in the 1940's. Among the architects who brought about the new trend in church architecture were Erich Mendelsohn, Barry Byrne, Frank Lloyd Wright, Mies Van der Rohe, Marcel Breuer, Pietro Belluschi, and Eliel and Eero Saarinen. The same emphasis on austerity and functionalism that dominated the design of the contemporary church in Europe was followed by these architects in America. Parabolic forms, the airplane hangar, and the tent are suggested by many designs, making the church no longer the principal landmark in the community. The use of modern building materials—concrete block, laminated wood, plastics, and the emphasis on the native qualities of materials—is the main source of aesthetic beauty in these churches. To beauty of proportion and design is added the beauty of color and light. Light is explored from the standpoint of modern technology, and both daylight and artificial light are used to accent the church services and give a mood of worship as well as to help express the theme of the architecture. Stained glass is used to temper the light. Abstract design and color in windows cut as Mondrian designs or whole walls of glass abstractions are more important than subject matter. Emil Frei, Robert Pinart, and Robert Sowers have done the stained glass in many of these churches. Contemporary churches in America have been built for the Lutherans by the Saarinens and by Belluschi. Other notable advances in modern American church design have been made in college chapels, of which the chapel at the Massachusetts Institute of Technology is the most interesting. Roman Catholic abbeys, of which that at Collegeville, Minnesota, is the most notable, have also embraced contemporary architecture and art. However, the Roman Catholic Church as a whole still builds traditional architecture, as evidenced by the new cathedrals in Baltimore and Washington. The Protestant Church is also behind the modern trend, and such cathedrals as Grace Cathedral in San Francisco and St. John the Divine in New York remain unfinished because of lack of courage to complete their design in contemporary terms.

To be sure, many new churches are being built in contemporary design all over the country. However, it would seem that it is from economic necessity instead of from preference, since they refuse to accept contemporary furnishings beyond architecture and stained glass. What is happening in most cases is a modernizing by means of light, carpeting, and draperies. The Presbyterian Church, Stamford, Connecticut, in the form of a fish, is a brave departure, but its uniqueness is mainly that of architecture and stained glass. Except for a few instances, nothing comparable to Coventry Cathedral or the French churches at Assy, Audincourt, Blois, or Vence, which are composite works of art, has been approached in America. However, St. Paul's Episcopal Church in Peoria, Illinois, comes as near to being a composite work of art as any church built in the twentieth century. From the beginning, Frederick Dunn, the architect, worked with painters, sculptors, and artist craftsmen. Zelda Strecker designed the wall behind the altar and the hand-printed vestments, and the sculptor Calvin Albert designed the bronze tabernacle, altar cross, and candlesticks. A sculptor also worked on the ceiling and the hand-carved altar, and the modern carpet with symbolical designs of the prairies was hand woven in Puerto Rico. Dunn also pioneered in simplicity and the use of artist craftsmen in the early 1940's when he designed the Episcopal Church of St. Luke, St. Louis, Missouri. The little chapel of the Blessed Sacrament at Stowe, Vermont, has windows and mural decorations by the artist André Girard, and St. Ann Chapel, Palo Alto, California, also has painted glass windows and Stations of the Cross by him as well. Other artists have also worked toward making the chapel a composite work of art. The mosaics on the baldachin over the altar and the Virgin of Lights are by Louisa Jenkins; the tabernacle and candlesticks were by the silversmith Victor Reis; and the silver crucifix is the work of Louis Féron.

In the last ten years the best-known American craftsmen have again been producing works with religious subject matter, and many of them are working on commissions for churches, although the church as a whole ignores significant art. The silversmiths Louis Féron, Ronald Pearson, Hudson Roysher, Victor Reis, and Ilse von Drage work almost exclusively on liturgical objects, including crosses, chalices, ciboriums, tabernacles, and monstrances. Other silversmiths who are known for this type of work include Harold Pride, Albino Manca, Jack Bowling, Harold Milbraith, Arthur Pulos, Rufus Jacoby, Philip Pavel, and Earl Krentzin. The well-known enamelers Kenneth Bates, Karl Drerup, and Edward Winter produce work with the jewel-like, precious qualities of antique enamels. Winter also experimented with steel, cast iron, and aluminum as bases for enamels on a large scale for murals for architectural decoration. Charles Bartley Jeffrey's enamels include crosses and a votive shrine, all small in scale and suitable for private devotion. Mary Ellen McDermott is one of the foremost designers of enamel plaques, crosses, panels, and reliquaries with religious subject matter. Virgil Cantini, Edris Eckhardt, and James Avery design enamel plaques, crosses, and candlesticks for the church, and Ronald Pearson and Ilse von Drage are also known for their enamelwork on crosses, chalices, and other liturgical objects.

Vestments in contemporary design with threads of gold and silver are woven by Barbara Markey. Gene Kavanaugh and William

Schickel design vestments with appliqué, and Sister Mary of the Compassion, O.P., designs and embroiders handmade vestments of contemporary design. The vestments of Father Edward Sutfin are made of sturdy textured material with bold color, and their design and style draw inspiration from early Byzantine mosaics.

American contemporary painters and sculptors are also interested and prepared to work for the contemporary church, although their art is not recognized or sought for by the Church. Modern sculpture, as in all past ages, is preoccupied with the relation of mass to space; and whether the sculpture be figurative or abstract, the material wood, stone, metal, plastic or wire, the interaction of volume and space is the sculptor's primary consideration. But in order to express a higher degree of intensity, the twentieth century sculptor has become an expressionist. He composes without sentiment or prettiness, simplifies and seeks the meaning beyond the surface as exemplified by the expressive sculptor Sahl Swarz, who works in the realm of the sacral. Donald Cook, in "The Four Horsemen," expresses the spirit of the Apocalyptic scripture. Nonfigurative sculptors work in organic abstractions, seeking forms and rhythms symbolizing the innate spiritual meanings and the essence of life in the nature of the materials themselves: the grain of the wood, the weight of the stone, and the malleable quality of metals and clay. Then there is an *avant-garde* of symbolic abstract expressionists. The most vital sculpture of this last group is being produced by the American sculptors, such as Calvin Albert, Herbert Ferber, Seymour Lipton, Abram Lassaw, and Jacques Lipchitz, who have executed commissioned sculpture for churches and synagogues. These abstract expressionists have interpreted religious symbols, going back to meanings related to the elements of fire, thunder, lightning, and the rainbow. Within this realm of space, silence, and elemental form lies the strength of contemporary religious sculpture.

The sculptor Mestrovic has a unique position in his dedication to sacred sculpture. His works range from a complete chapel to individual works for churches, such as a crucifix, the Madonna and Child, a pietà, figures of saints, Job, John the Baptist, and such subjects as "Supplication." Mestrovic expresses suffering, anguish, and hope by means of drapery, gesture, the position of the head, and long, expressive hands. His power, originality, and heroic concept put him at the top of the list of present-day figurative sculptors.

Mestrovic's comments about his early "Crucifixion" may be an aid to understanding art that we do not like or comprehend: "I carved in wood the scene of the crucifixion. Many people did not like it because it was not aesthetically pleasing. They found the crucified Christ too emaciated and disfigured. But the crucifixion scene was not meant to represent the historical Jesus nor His supreme sacrifice. It was intended to depict the crucifixion of His idea, the perversion and disfiguration of the teachings for which He came into this world and for which He died on the cross."

Another present-day sculptor who has worked for the Church and whose unique talent has assigned him a place among the greats is Jacques Lipchitz. Lipchitz works in the expressive manner of Rodin and with the eloquence of Bernini, and his subject matter includes monumental allegories such as "Jacob Wrestling with the Angel," and "The Prodigal Son," and the figure of "Notre-Dame de Liesse" for the church at Assy, France.

Much of the art of the twentieth century Christian painter is social and revolutionary. Christ is made the Victim, and He is identified with the poor and the distressed. Society is depicted as brutal, callous, and indifferent. In José Orozco's "Christ Destroying the Cross," Christ condemns the world and its present Christianity.

Foremost among the advance guard of American painters who work with an intensely religious overtone is Abraham Rattner. His religious subjects represent man and his sufferings, not the Church. His "Job" is the suffering and anguish of mankind. Design and color work together to express his philosophic and aesthetic goals. In "The Last Judgment" his religious symbolism reaches a climax. It is an apocalyptic vision of terror and wonder expressed in terms of the Atomic Age, and the luminous glow of its color has the elemental quality of fire. Rico Lebrun paints the Passion of Christ not as a devotional theme, but to obtain the universal by means of terror and pity. The series culminates in his "Crucifixion," which is one of the most significant contemporary paintings. In order to reestablish the real meaning of the scene, Lebrun brutalizes his figures to strike horror into the spectator.

Dali, too, has upset the conventions of religious art. Yet he paints with sincerity, reverence, and an intense mystical realism that make the everyday object extraordinary. In his portrayal of the discontinuance of matter and the disintegration of the body, he deals in nuclear physics to bring an understanding of the miraculous mysticism of religion. Dali assembles a Cross of cubes surrounding the bread of the Holy Eucharist to remind us of an atomic pile and "suggest a mystical link which must sooner or later bind our discoveries in nuclear physics to religious concepts."

Kelly Fearing and Fred Nagler deal with religious matter in the modern figurative sense. Fearing uses the lyrical backgrounds of nature—rocks, trees, clouds, and sky—to create other-world settings for his figures of saints and Old Testament characters. Nagler's religious paintings have a sincerity, compassion, and intensity of feeling. He has painted modern conceptions of the Last Supper, Crucifixion, Madonnas, and portraits of Christ. His paintings, although they depart from tradition, are not radical treatments of the subjects. Nagler works almost exclusively in the religious theme, but only recently has his work found its way into churches. Robert Motherwell has done commissioned works for churches in the contemporary language of color and line. Seymour Fogel discards the representational image and seeks to communicate mood and feeling to increase and intensify religious feeling. William Congdon, one of America's most-gifted abstract expressionists, has also recently been employing his abstract technique to express deeply felt religious subject matter. These are a few of the outstanding American painters and sculptors who work almost exclusively in the religious field, even though they receive few commissions from the Church.

The Pennell Collection at the Library of Congress in Washington, and the Sloniker Collection in the Cincinnati Art Museum, include woodcuts, wood engravings, lithographs, serigraphs, etchings, and engravings by leading twentieth century artists, all dealing with Biblical and religious themes. Although secular subjects and abstract themes have dominated the art of our century, the Old and New Testaments and the lives of the saints have continued to fire the imagination of many of these leading graphic artists. Nearly half of the subjects depicted are drawn from the life of Christ, but there are also representations of such Old Testament figures as Adam and Eve, Tobias and the angel, Jonah and the whale, and the Shulamite of the Song of Solomon. Saints portrayed include St. Anthony, St. Christopher, St. Francis, St. George, and St. Sebastian. Among American artists represented are Leonard Baskin, Sister Mary Corita, Rudy Pozzatti, Benton Spruance, André Racz, Gabor Peterdi, June Wayne, and Mauricio Lasansky. Artists from abroad are also shown, including Ernst Barlach, Marc Chagall, Salvador

Dali, James Ensor, José Clemente Orozco, and Georges Rouault. But there are many other artists who choose religious subjects to express their search for the universal. Indeed, there are many signs today that point to a revival of Church art. It first of all manifests itself in the personal expression of artists. The writings and sayings of contemporary artists reveal their innate religion, although it may not conform to the formality of sect or creed. There is a force at work drawing art back to the great subjects and motifs of Christian faith, and the artist seeks an encounter with the sacred and a concern with man's inner soul.

But what of the Church? The nature and task of Church art is as much a question of religion as it is of art. If we demand faith and sincerity on the part of the artist, does it not also behoove the Church to approach art with some understanding? The indifference and lack of appreciation of art by the clergy has led to the use of works of art that do not even represent the Christian Faith. Churches are furnished and decorated from church-supply catalogues or by decorators and second-rate artists who turn out works full of sentiment and cheap symbolism. Indeed, one of the great tragedies of today is that Church art is available but has not found its way into the church. One basic reason for this is that artistic instruction has no place in the curriculum of the theological seminarian, yet many of these men will later have to direct the building of new churches or repair and redecorate old ones.

The question of Church art goes much deeper than the Church admits. It is not a question of teaching the history of religion. It is the fundamentals of the Faith that must be articulated, and if they are to be understood today they must be expressed in the language of the present.

The contemporary Church, whatever its faith or denomination, should have a living art. This does not mean that the art should be lifelike; on the contrary, for lifelike naturalism says too much, as does realistic and narrative art. All epochs of original art recognized a divorce between the forms of reality and the forms of art. Christian art must be honest; it must be able to express the human situation as the artist and the culture of today see it. We must admit that neither naturalism nor idealism expresses the contemporary scene. If today's world is beset with radical destructive trends, we must have the strength to encounter them and to protest and to find beneath them all the deep everlasting realities of the ultimate and infinite. Today's religious art should not only express and reflect religious life; it should ennoble and strengthen everyday life, transmute the natural into the spiritual, and relate the past to the present. This cannot be done by looking backward and imitating the artistic styles of the past. Contemporary Church art must have its own moment of creative ecstasy if it is to live in the twentieth century. The Church cannot offer the twentieth century the image it offered the nineteenth century. It can no longer quote Thomas Aquinas, Luther, and Calvin as if nothing had happened since their time, and Church art can no longer peddle Hofmann, Holman Hunt, and Plockhorst, or even the old masters, as though they represented the only sacred artistic style. Christian art is not Gothic, as so many people like to think. Nor is it narrative or representational or as sentimental as our Sunday-school cards teach. Christianity claims to be the Truth, not Reality. Thus if the true life be portrayed it must break free from the real and from illustrative realistic art. Christianity looks toward the world to come, and the task of the Christian artist must be to portray his subject so that it partakes of the unseen values of the other world. It must show the universal in the time-bound event. It must show but not describe. It must convey the symbol, not the fact. "We look not at the things which are seen."

It is not for the artist to create new symbols. A "new look" is not the answer, but a new approach, a reshaping and creating of new combinations to regenerate the original power of the traditional symbol and to give new life to age-old truths. The artist should strive again to set afire the part of religion that morality and too much analysis have smothered. Art can restore the mystical, the sense of wonder, and the moving traditional religion that is not just of the intellect but of the senses—eyes, ears, touch, and movement. "That which from the beginning, which we have heard, which we have seen with our eyes, which we have looked upon and touched with our hands, concerning the word of life" (I John 1:1).

Today we need symbols designed and executed so that they are beautiful in themselves and so that when we look at them we can again grasp their original meanings. We also need new symbols for the new Church of today—symbols that are universal and can be used by all churches. Not only traditional Christian symbols and Biblical scenes, but even dogma can be studied so that we may

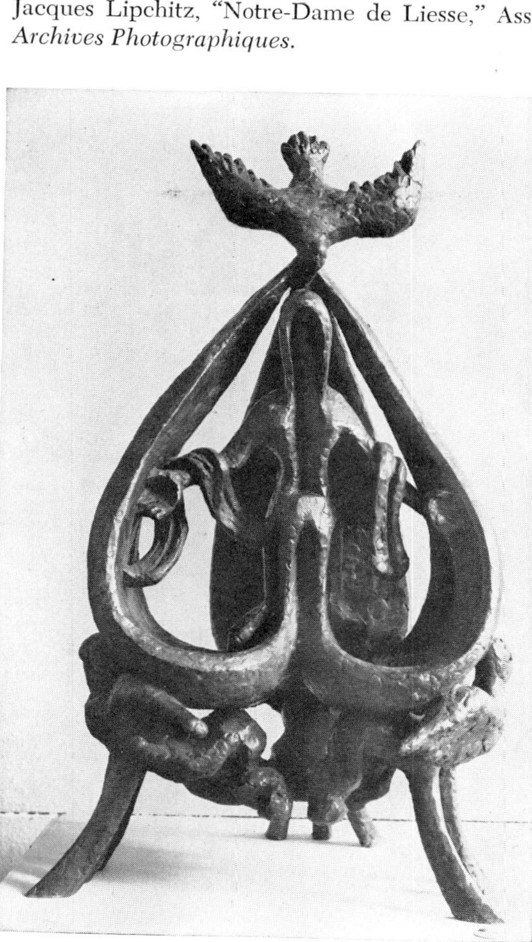

Jacques Lipchitz, "Notre-Dame de Liesse," Assy. *Archives Photographiques.*

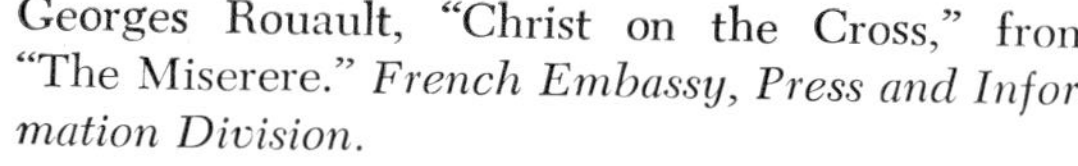

Georges Rouault, "Christ on the Cross," from "The Miserere." *French Embassy, Press and Information Division.*

Opposite: Bronze processional cross by Mataré.

Notre-Dame de Royan, Guillaume Gillet, architect. The austere form is relieved by the panels of stained glass. *French Cultural Services.*

Bronze door at the Marketkirche, Hanover, Germany, by Gerhard Marcks. Above is a risen Christ; below are scenes from contemporary life. *Galerie Rudolf Hoffmann.*

PLATE LII

PLATE LIII

"Ecce Homo," by Jacob Epstein. *British Information Service.*

Opposite: Gerald Benney's silver reredos with silver-gilt cross and candlesticks, especially commissioned by the Worshipful Company of Goldsmiths, London. *Photo British Artists Craftsmen.*

Opposite: Cathedral of St. Michael, Coventry. Photograph of the inside of the model, looking toward the altar and the tapestry designed by Graham Sutherland and now being woven in Aubusson by Pinton Frères. The architect is Sir Basil Spence. *Photo Alfred Cracknell.*

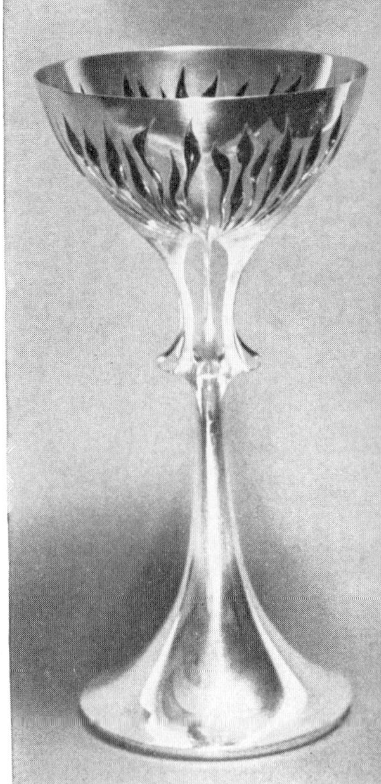

Ronald Pearson's chalice with silver and plique-à-jour. *Collection of Museum of Contemporary Crafts.*

"Disciple," detail of copper repoussé cross by Jean de Marco. *Jean de Marco and National Sculpture Society.*

The Chapel of Portsmouth Priory School: the architectural form allows for a central altar above which hangs a metal sculpture by Richard Lippold. Light is the dominating factor. Pietro Belluschi, architect. *Photo John T. Hopf.*

St. Paul's Episcopal Church, Peoria, Illinois, Frederick Dunn, architect, showing the interior, center altar with dome lighting, and chapel beyond with walls of contemporary symbols in squares. *Photo* Peoria Journal Star.

Exterior of St. Paul's Episcopal Church, Peoria, Illinois. The stained glass is by Emil Frei.

St. Paul's Episcopal Church, Peoria, Illinois. The entrance shows the front wall of contemporary glass by Emil Frei, with organ and font. *Photo G. E. Mortimer.*

PLATE LVII

Chapel altar cross in bronze, St. Paul's Church, Peoria, Illinois, by Calvin Albert.

Silver crucifix by Louis Féron, silversmith.

Ivan Mestrovic, "Gethsemane," wood carving. *National Sculpture Society.*

Abraham Rattner, "The Last Judgment," Triptych, 1953-1956. *The Downtown Gallery.*

Salvador Dali, "The Sacrament of the Last Supper." A combination of symbolism and realism draws the spectator into the picture. The dodecahedron is the Greek symbol of the universe. The two arms are a segment of a circle, and a second arc is formed by the heads of the communicants. *National Gallery of Art, Washington, D.C.*

Rico Lebrun's "The Crucifixion." *Syracuse University Collection.*

A Mighty Fortress: First Lutheran Church, Kennewick, Washington. Durham, Anderson, and Freed, architects. *Photo Charles R. Pearson.*

St. Edmund's Church, Elm Grove, Wisconsin, William P. Wenzler, architect, relates to the space age. The roof line suggests airplane wings. *Photo Big Cedar Studios.*

penetrate fundamental hidden ideas more profoundly. But such ideas must be stripped of their old sentimental storytelling qualities. This can and has been done without loss of their universal significance or supernatural value. "The Crucifixion" in the Cathedral of St. Andrew in Port-au-Prince, Haiti, the "Yellow Christ" of Gauguin, "The Last Supper" of Stanley Spencer, and the lyrical "Annunciation" of Lauren Ford are all clothed in the habits of the here and now, yet the story is no less dignified when described in the contemporary vocabulary instead of in Renaissance or Victorian language.

If we grant that religious art must be in tune with present-day life, then it must be articulated in one of the art forms of the twentieth century, not in archaic or nineteenth century vesture. Many art styles exist today, but the old worn styles are out of touch with their sources, and their traditional settings are out of rhythm with both life and religion. But there are new art styles that speak the contemporary language, and it is these new styles that religion must embrace and purify for use in the Church.

The most important element in contemporary art is the expressive element. The expressive element is not new. It has been present in all periods of great religious art and in the work of great religious artists from the art of the catacombs through Byzantine, Romanesque, Gothic, Renaissance, and Baroque, to Georges Rouault. Expressionism in art corresponds to the ecstatic spiritual type of religious experience. Its rediscovery came after the impressionists, when a few radical artists led by Cézanne gave up the convention of imitation. Expressionism does not imitate or illustrate. It changes the appearance of ordinary things so that they are different from what they appear to be in nature. It seeks to express the unseen meaning beneath the surface or the soul of the object. The inspiration for expressive art often comes from the memory of an event rather than from observation. This produces a subjective feeling and a dimension of depth in an expressive work of art. There is ever the search for the intense feeling and for the eternal rather than the passing value. The expressive artist explores his mind and subconscious emotions, and his search for self-realization and truth has led him to the church structure as the greatest place in which to express his abilities. His new-found power not only makes him able to fashion the traditional symbolisms and images demanded by the Church but also to create his own feelings of exaltation and belief, and, by the psychological use of color and form, contribute to the mood and spiritual tone of the church building and bring it into harmony with the Church service. By this communicative use, contemporary art can relate to religion. In expressive religious art we are not particularly interested in the subject matter, but in how it is expressed and what aesthetic and religious emotions and abstract truths it has been able to communicate. If we approach this art as visual music, and look for the rhythmic harmony of line, dark and light masses, and color, we can learn to appreciate art that we may not fully understand. But if the artist is to retain his rightful place in society, he must remain readable without becoming imitative, and to do so he must retain some fragments of representation. Modern workers in stained glass have solved this problem by creating religious still lifes. Léger has done so in his series of stained-glass windows at Audincourt; Henry Lee Willet and others have done it in concrete-glass compositions in American churches; and the artist Alfred Manessier has done it in his paintings.

The abstract artist claims a spiritual significance for his work. A work of art is "a hymn of praise" and "their prayer is in the practise of their trade" (Ecclesiasticus 38:34). If the artist has religious sensibility, his work can do much for religion. Often the artist depending on his own sensibility and artistic vision is nearer to doctrinal accuracy than theologians who do not really see his work. Without understanding their complete significance, the contemporary non-Christian artist is turning to Christian themes, and his approach is predominantly spiritual because of pure design, abstract structure, expression of inner feelings and emotions, or of a mystic dream world beyond the real.

Thus contemporary art is able to make a setting for the liturgy which is itself built on an abstract aesthetic structure. If one listens to the reading of the Bible or the Eucharistic service, even in a language one does not understand, the beauty of the structure will be felt. The beauty of certain phrases, the repetition, the rhythm, the contrasts, and the unity of composition are all there as in a great painting or musical composition. Such phrases as "Holy, Holy, Holy," the "Gloria," and "Amen," or the "Blessed" of the Beatitudes create beauty by means of rhythmic repetition. Indeed, the beauty of words and phrases and prescribed gesture in the liturgy is such that it is difficult for even a pedestrian priest to destroy their beauty. Liturgy was not made, however, for the pleasure of forming beautiful symbols, language, or gestures, but for a spiritual need, and when this is accomplished the result is beauty. Art in harmony with the beauty of the liturgy can help create the atmosphere and furnish illustration and accompaniment to worship. Thus sacred art can be made a form of worship.

The mystery of the liturgy is expressed through symbol that leaves much unsaid. The economy or restraint of symbolic art is the sphere of the contemporary artist, for he can communicate much by means of restraint. In past ages the Church accepted both simplification and distortion in art, and these characteristics of contemporary art should not be objected to. In fact, the chief objection to contemporary art is its dehumanization. Though man is no longer the center of interest in any style of contemporary art, is this not a reflection of the tragic dehumanization of present-day life that the artist perceives even while we seek to hide it? The attempt to show the infinite by annihilating reality can lead to works in which nothing is expressed, but it can also lead to mystical religious art. Art shows that awe, wonder, and worship can be aroused by color, line, and nonrealistic forms. These are the factors that have helped to keep religion alive through the ages. Matter can express the things of the spirit, but a sublime or mystical quality is more important. Art must show the joy and the glory of the Cross. The mission of contemporary Christian art should be to keep alive the wonder and mystery of the unknown that has given the mystical, awe-inspiring, numinous quality to all great religious art and that proclaims, "Our God is a great God."

Bibliography

General

John Canady, *Mainstreams of Modern Art*. Simon & Schuster, New York, 1959.
Sheldon Cheney, *A World History of Art*. Viking Press, New York, 1956.
Maurice Denis, *Histoire d'art religieux*. Paris, Flammarion.
Elie Faure, *The Spirit of the Forms*. Harper & Brothers, New York, 1930.
Helen Gardner, *Art Through the Ages*. Harcourt, Brace, New York, 1959.
Arnold Hauser, *The Social History of Art*. Alfred A. Knopf, New York, 1951.
René Huyghe, *Ideas and Images in World Art*. Harry N. Abrams, Inc., New York, 1959.
Martin Hürlimann and Eric Newton, *Masterpieces of European Sculpture*. Harry N. Abrams, Inc., New York, 1959.
N. Pevsner, *An Outline of European Architecture*, Penguin Books, New York, 1960.
F. J. Roos, Jr., *An Illustrated Handbook of Art History*. The Macmillan Company, New York, 1954.
William Osborne Taylor, *The Emergence of Christian Culture in the West*, Harper Torch Books, New York.
Heinrich Wölfflin, *Principles of Art History*. Dover Press, New York, 1950.

Iconography

A. M. Didron, *Christian Iconography*, 2 vols. George Bell & Sons, London, 1886.
Anna Brownell Jameson, *Legends of the Madonna; Sacred and Legendary Art; History of Our Lord*. Longmans, Green & Co., 1872.
Norman Laliberte and Edward N. West, *The History of the Cross*. The Macmillan Company, New York, 1960.
Emile Mâle, *Religious Art*. Noonday Press, New York, 1958.
——, *Gothic Image*. Harper, New York, 1958.
André Malraux, *The Metamorphosis of the Gods*. Doubleday & Company, Garden City, New York, 1960.
Erwin Panofsky, *Studies in Iconography*. Oxford University Press, New York, 1939.
Louis Reau, *Iconographie de l'art Chrétien*, 4 vols. Presses Universitaires de France, 1955–1959.
E. Baldwin Smith, *Architectural Symbolism of Imperial Rome and the Middle Ages*. Princeton University Press, 1956.
Paul Thoby, *Le Crucifix des origines au Council de Trente*. Bellanger, Nantes, 1959.
Evelyn J. Vavala, *Le Croce dipint a Italianae: l'iconografia della Passione*. Casa editrice Apollo, Verone, 1929.
Maurice Vloberg, *L'Eucharistie dans l'art*. B. Arthaud, 1946.

Arthur Watson, *The Early Iconography of the Tree of Jesse*. Oxford University Press, London, 1934.

Symbolism

LeRoy H. Appleton and Stephen Bridges, *Symbolism in Liturgical Art*. Charles Scribner's Sons, New York, 1959.

George Ferguson, *Signs and Symbols in Christian Art*. Oxford University Press, New York, 1959.

Elizabeth Goldsmith, *Sacred Symbols in Art*. G. P. Putnam's Sons, New York, 1912.

Elizabeth Haig, *Floral Symbolism of the Great Masters*. Kegan Paul, Trench, Trubner & Co., Ltd., London, 1913.

Aesthetics, Art Appreciation, and Criticism

Philip C. Beam, *The Language of Art*. Ronald Press, New York, 1958.

Clive Bell, *Art*. Putnam-Capricorn Books, New York, 1959.

Bernard Berenson, *Aesthetics and History in the Visual Arts*. Pantheon, New York, 1948.

François Cali, *The Architecture of Truth*. G. Braziller, London, 1957.

R. G. Collingwood, *The Principles of Art*. Oxford University Press, 1938.

John Dewey, *Art as Experience*. G. P. Putnam's Sons, Inc., New York, 1934.

Henri Focillon, *The Life of Forms in Art*. George Wittenborn, New York, 1948.

Roger Fry, *Vision and Design*. Brentano, New York, 1924.

Etienne Gilson, *Painting and Reality*. Pantheon Books, New York, 1957.

Theodore Meyer Greene, *The Arts and the Art of Criticism*. Princeton University Press, 1940.

G. W. F. Hegel, *The Philosophy of Fine Art*, 4 vols. G. G. Bell & Sons, Ltd., London, 1920.

Patrick Heron, *The Changing Forms of Art*. The Macmillan Company, New York, 1956.

Suzanne Langer, *Feeling and Form*. Charles Scribner's Sons, New York, 1953.

Jacques Maritain, *Art and Scholasticism*. Charles Scribner's Sons, New York, 1954.

Rudolf Otto, *The Idea of the Holy*. Oxford University Press, London, 1928.

S. C. Pepper, *Principles of Art Appreciation*. Harcourt, Brace & Co., New York, 1949.

Arthur Pope, *The Language of Drawing and Painting*. Cambridge University Press, New York, 1949.

Herbert Read, *The Meaning of Art*. Penguin Books, New York, 1959.

George Santayana, *The Sense of Beauty*. Charles Scribner's Sons, New York, 1896.

Robert Sencourt, *The Consecration of Genius*. Hollis & Carter, London, 1947.

Early Christian

O. M. Dalton, *East Christian Art*. Oxford University Press, 1925.

J. G. Davies, *Origin of Early Christian Architecture*. Philosophical Library, New York, 1953.

G. Duthuit, *La Sculpture copte.* G. van Oest, Paris, 1931.

Arthur L. Frothingham, *Monuments of Christian Rome.* The Macmillan Company, New York, 1908.

Françoise Henry, *Early Christian Irish Art.* C. O'Lochaimm, 1954.

Dow Levi, *Antioch Mosaic Pavements.* Princeton University Press, 1947.

Walter Lowrie, *Art in the Early Church.* Pantheon Books, New York, 1947.

Charles R. Morey, *Early Christian Art.* Princeton University Press, 1953.

J. Natanson, *Early Christian Ivories.* A. Tiranti, London, 1953.

D. Talbot Rice, *The Beginnings of Christian Art.* Abingdon Press, Nashville, 1958.

Joseph Strzygowski, *Origin of Christian Church Art.* Oxford University Press, 1923.

K. Weitzmann, *Illustrations in Roll and Codex.* Princeton Univ. Press, 1947.

——, *The Joshua Roll.* Princeton University Press, 1948.

Thomas Whittimore, *The Mosaics of S. Sophia at Istanbul,* 4 vols. Oxford, 1933–1952.

Joseph Wilpert, *Roma sotterranea: le pitture delle catacombe romane.* Desclee, Lefebre & Co., Roma, 1903.

——, *Die Römischen Mosäiken und Malereien der kirchenlichen Bauten vom IV bis XIII,* 4 vols. Herder & Co., Freiburg, 1924.

——, *I. Sarcofagi cristiani antichi,* 3 vols. Pontificio Institudodi Archeologia Cristiana, Roma, 1929–1932.

Byzantine

O. M. Dalton, *Byzantine Art and Archaeology.* Oxford, 1911.

André Grabar, *Byzantine Painting.* Skira, 1953.

Alfred Maskell, *Ivories.* Methuen & Co., London, 1905.

A. Pierce and R. Tyler, *Art Byzantine.* Ernest Benn, Ltd., 1926.

D. Talbot Rice, *Byzantine Art.* Penguin Books, New York, 1954.

Romanesque

Edgar Waterman Anthony, *Romanesque Frescoes.* Princeton University Press, 1951.

Arthur Clapham, *Romanesque Architecture in Western Europe.* Clarendon Press, Oxford, 1936.

Hans Decker, *Romanesque Art in Italy.* Harry N. Abrams, New York, 1959.

Paul Deschamps, *French Sculpture of the Romanesque Period.* Panthéon Firenz-Pegasus, Paris, 1930.

Joan Evans, *Cluniac Art of the Romanesque Period.* Cambridge University Press, 1958.

André Grabar, *Early Medieval Painting.* Skira, 1957.

M. R. James, *The Apocalypse in Art.* Oxford University Press, 1931.

T. D. Kendrick, *Anglo-Saxon Art.* Methuen & Co., London, 1938.

Herman Leisinger, *Romanische Bronzen: Kirchenfüren im mittelalterlichen Europa.* Europa Verlag, 1956.

André Lejard, *Les Tapis d'Apocalypse de la Cathédrale d'Angers.* A. Michel, Paris, 1942.

Arthur Kingsley Porter, *Romanesque Sculpture of the Pilgrimage Roads.* Marshall Jones, Boston, 1923.

Hans Swarzenki, *Monuments of Romanesque.* Chicago University Press, 1954.

Emile van Moe, *L'Apocalypse de S. Sever.* Edition de Cluny, Paris, 1943.

Gothic

Hugh Arnold, *Stained Glass of the Middle Ages in England and France.* The Macmillan Company, New York, 1939.

Marcel Aubert, *French Sculpture at the Beginning of the Gothic Period.* Pantheon Books, 1929.

Bernard Berenson, *Studies in Medieval Painting.* Oxford University Press, 1930.

M. Chamot, *English Medieval Enamels.* E. Benn, London, 1930.

Charles J. Connick, *Adventures in Light and Color.* Random House, 1937.

Jacques Dupont and Cesare Gnudi, *Gothic Painting.* Skira, 1954.

Joan Evans, *English Art: 1307–1461.* Oxford University Press, 1949.

John Harvey, *The Gothic World.* B. T. Batsford, London, 1950.

W. R. Lethaby, *Medieval Art from the Peace of the Church to the Eve of the Renaissance.* Philosophical Library, 1950.

Emile Mâle, *The Gothic Image.* Harper Torch Book, New York, 1958.

G. Marchini, *Stained Glass in Italy.* Harry N. Abrams, New York, 1957.

C. R. Morey, *Medieval Art.* W. W. Norton Co., New York, 1942.

Erwin Panofsky, *Early Netherlandish Painting.* Harvard University Press, 1954.

——, *Gothic Architecture and Scholasticism.* Arch Abbey Press, Pa., 1951.

John Pope-Hennessy, *Italian Gothic Sculpture.* Phaidon, 1955.

O. Siren, *Giotto and Some of His Followers.* Harvard University Press, 1917.

Baron Joseph van der Elst, *The Last Flowering of the Middle Ages.* Doubleday, New York, 1944.

Otto von Simon, *The Gothic Cathedral,* Pantheon, 1956.

Renaissance

Guilia Argan, *Botticelli.* Skira, 1957.

O. Benesch, *Art of the Renaissance in Northern Europe.* Harvard University Press, 1945.

Bernard Berenson, *Italian Painters of the Renaissance.* Phaidon, 1952.

——, *Piero della Francesca.* Macmillan, London, 1954.

Charles De Tolnay, *Michelangelo,* 6 vols. Princeton University Press, 1945–1961.

Ludwig Heydenreich, *Leonardo da Vinci.* The Macmillan Company, New York, 1955.

H. W. Janson, *The Sculpture of Donatello.* Princeton University Press, 1957.

Richard Krautheimer, *Ghiberti.* Princeton University Press, 1956.

Jacques Lassaigne and Guilo Carlo Argan, *The Fifteenth Century, from Van Eyck to Botticelli.* Skira, 1955.

V. Moschini, *Giambellini.* Istituto Italiano di Arti Grafichi, Bergamo, 1943.

Erwin Panofsky, *Albert Dürer*. Princeton University Press, 1955.
John Pope-Hennessy, *Fra Angelico*, Phaidon Press, 1953.
——, *Italian Renaissance Sculpture*. Phaidon Press, 1958.
Filippo Rossi, *Italian Jeweled Arts*. Harry N. Abrams, New York, 1957.
W. E. Suida, *Raphael*. Phaidon Press, 1948.
Wylie Sypher, *Four Stages of Renaissance Style*. Doubleday Anchor Books, 1955.
Hans Tietze, *Tintoretto*. Phaidon Press, 1948.
——, *Titian*. Phaidon Press, 1950.
Tietze-Courat, *Mantegna*. Phaidon Press, 1955.
Lionello Venturi, *Sixteenth Century Painting*. Skira, 1956.
R. Wittkower, *The Architectural Principles in the Age of Humanism*. A. Tiranti, London, 1952.

Baroque

Francisco Abbad-Ríos, *Las Immaculades de Murillo*. Barcelona, 1948.
John Bourke, *Baroque Churches of Central Europe*. Faber and Faber, London, 1958.
Joseph Braun, *Die Kirchenbauten der Deutschen Jesuiten*. Freiburg, 1908–1910.
G. G. Coulton, *Art and the Reformation*. Cambridge University Press, 1953.
Joseph Crouch, *Puritanism and Art*. Cassell, London, 1910.
Arthur L. Drummond, *Architecture of Protestantism*. Edinburgh, 1934.
Jacques Dupont, *Seventeenth Century Painting*. Skira, 1951.
T. H. Fokker, *Poussin*, München, 1914.
——, *Roman Baroque Art*. Oxford University Press, London, 1938.
W. Friedlander, *Caravaggio Studies*. Princeton University Press, 1955.
Karl Holl, *The Cultural Significance of the Reformation*. Merdian, New York, 1959.
Pál Kelemen, *Baroque and Rococo in Latin America*. The Macmillan Company, New York, 1951.
B. Knipping, *De Iconografie van de Contra Reformatie in de Nederlander*, 2 vols. Hilversun, 1939–1940.
Jacques Lassaigne, *Spanish Painting*. Skira, 1952.
M. D. Molesworth, *English Baroque, Rococo and Neoclassical*. Victoria and Albert Museum, 1954.
James Lees Milne, *Baroque in Italy*. The Macmillan Company, New York, 1959.
——, *Gian Lorenzo Bernini: Sculptor of Roman Baroque*. Phaidon Press, 1955.
W. A. Visser 't Hooft, *Rembrandt and the Gospel*. Westminster Press, Philadelphia, 1958.
Marcus Whiffen, *Stuart and Georgian Churches. B. T.* Batsford, 1948.

Nineteenth Century

Peter Anson, *Fashions in Church Furnishings: 1840–1940*. The Macmillan Company, 1960.

Basil F. Clarke, *Church Builders of the Nineteenth Century.* The Macmillan Company, 1938.

G. Hay, *Architecture of Scottish Post-Reformation Churches.* Oxford University Press, 1957.

Henry Russell Hitchcock, *Early Victorian Architecture in Great Britain.* Yale University Press, 1954.

Holman W. Hunt, *Pre-Raphaelitism,* 2 vols. The Macmillan Company, New York, 1905.

Robin Ironside, *Pre-Raphaelite Painters.* Phaidon Press, 1948.

Richard Muther, *The History of Modern Painting,* Dutton, 1907.

A. Welby Pugin, *Designs for Gold and Silversmiths.* Ackermann, London, 1836.

——, *Floriated Ornament.* G. H. Bohn, London, 1849.

J. Ruskin, *The Lamp of Beauty.* Phaidon Press, 1959.

Joseph C. Sloane, *French Painting Between Past and Present.* Princeton University Press, 1951.

Contemporary

Roberto Aloi, *Esempi di decorazione moderna di tutto il mondo.* Ulrico Hoepli Editore, Milano, 1950.

Beryl Dean, *Ecclesiastical Embroidery.* Batsford, 1958.

Anton Henze, *Contemporary Church Art.* Sheed & Ward, New York, 1956.

Kirchengerat: *Jahrbuch für Christliche Künst, 1957–1958.* München.

Katharine Morrison McClinton, *The Changing Church.* Morehouse-Gorham, Inc., New York, 1957.

Joan Morris, *Modern Sacred Art.* Sands & Co., London, 1938.

Andrew Carnduff Ritchie, *Sculpture of the Twentieth Century.* Museum of Modern Art, New York, 1952.

Sculpture of Mestrovic. Syracuse University Press, 1948.

Plastik im Kirchenbau: Jahrbuch für Christliche Künst, 1955–1956. München.

Rudolf Schwarz, *The Church Incarnate.* Henry Regnery, 1958.

Hans Sedlmayr, *Art in Crisis.* Henry Regnery, New York, 1958.

R. H. Wilenski, *The Meaning of Modern Sculpture.* Faber and Faber, London, 1932.

Magazines

Art Chrétien, Paris, France
Arte Cristiana, Milan, Italy
Art d'Eglise, Bruges, Belgium
Arte Sacre, Turin, Italy
L'Art Sacré, Paris, France
L'Artisan et l'art liturgique, Utrecht, Holland
Christliche Künstblätter, Linz, Austria
Liturgical Arts, New York
National Sculpture Review, winter issues
Church Building, New York

Index